115
Saintly Fun Facts

 daring deeds

 heroic happenings

 serendipitous surprises

FOR KIDS OF ALL AGES

by Bernadette McCarver Snyder

LIGUORI
PUBLICATIONS

One Liguori Drive
Liguori, MO 63057-9999
(314) 464-2500

Imprimi Potest:
James Shea, C.SS.R.
Provincial, St. Louis Province
The Redemptorists

Imprimatur:
Monsignor Maurice F. Byrne
Vice Chancellor, Archdiocese of St. Louis

ISBN 0-89243-562-3
Library of Congress Catalog Card Number: 93-78618

Cover and interior art by Chris Sharp

Dedication

I dedicate this book to my "saintly" family, who have long suffered through my writer's moods and musings; to my "saintly" friends (especially Mary Clare Geerling), who have patiently listened to more than their share of *Fun Facts;* to the "saintly" editors, artists, secretaries, and critics, who have helped shape my books; and to my own special saints, Saint Bernadette and our Blessed Mother Mary. Holy Halo! Thanks to all.

Contents

Introduction

Do you know any saints? Well, maybe you don't. Or maybe you DO!

Do you know what a saint IS? Well, maybe you do. Or maybe you DON'T!

Do you think a saint could only be a person who lived on earth many, many years ago and did nothing but pray all day and never had any fun? Or do you think a saint could be a hero who traveled around the world, lived a life full of surprises and discoveries, and had adventures even more dangerous and exciting than "pretend" heroes like Superman or Wonder Woman?

Do you think saints only lived yesterday? Or could there be saints on earth today? Could one be living in your city or your neighborhood or maybe even in your house?

Could a saint be somebody just like you?

Well, there are ALL KINDS of saints. Some are "official" saints who have been honored by the Church. Some are good and holy people who may pray a lot OR work hard to help others OR take risks to change things so the world can be a better place.

Think about the people you know and how they live. Do you know any saintly people? And what about YOU? Maybe YOU are a saint "in training"!

This book will give you a better idea of what a "saint" is. So turn the page and read about daring deeds and heroic happenings. And discover some strange but "saintly" fun facts!

Preface

Attention! Attention! Before you start reading, wait a minute!

Do you know what a PATRON saint is? Maybe you do but just in case you don't, you might WANT to know because a lot of them are mentioned in this book.

You probably know that a "patron" is someone who encourages, helps, or protects someone else. A "patron" of the arts might be someone who gives money to an art museum or volunteers to work there for free—to HELP people learn about art. A "patron" might pay the tuition for a poor student or give money to help support a struggling writer. A "patron" who is a scientist or a mathematician or a baseball player might give advice and encouragement and/or private instruction to help a BEGINNING scientist or mathematician or baseball player.

Well, a "patron" saint is one who has been designated by the Church to help YOU whenever you have a particular problem. You can ask the saint to "intercede," or run interference, for you! You can ask the saint to ask God to help you when you are in some kind of trouble or just if you are doing some special kind of work. There are patron saints for actors and architects, bankers and barrel makers, someone who is in danger of drowning or endangered by a dog bite, someone who has been falsely accused, or someone who works on a farm! There's a patron saint for just about anybody and everybody.

Through the centuries, some of the saints have become patrons of some very strange things. For example, Saint Agatha is the patron saint of people who are afraid of volcanoes! You'll probably never have a problem with volcanoes, but just in case you do, now you know Saint Agatha is the one to ask for help!

No one is really sure why Saint Agatha became a volcano patron, but she DID live in Sicily, Italy, and that's where a famous active volcano, known as Mount Etna, often blasts off, spewing out fire and hot lava. It might be exciting to WATCH a volcano shooting off fireworks on TV, but if you LIVED near it, that would be very scary and dangerous. So the people there probably prayed for this popular Italian saint to ask God to help them—and that's how Saint Agatha became a volcano patron!

You might be interested to know that the patron saint of writers is Saint Francis de Sales, but there are SEVERAL saints who are patrons of young people—including Saint John Bosco, Raphael the Archangel, and Saint Stanislaus Kostka.

You say you've never heard of Saint Stanislaus Kostka? Well, then, read on!

Adelaide

This saint lived a "good news-bad news" life!

Good news! When she was sixteen years old, Adelaide married King Lothair of Italy and became a queen. Bad news! Only three years later, Lothair died—and it was rumored that he had been POISONED by a man named Berengarius. Berengarius took over the kingdom and threw Adelaide into prison!

Good news! Within a year, the German King Otto invaded and won the kingdom, freed Adelaide from prison, and married her! They had three sons and were married for over twenty years. Adelaide was very intelligent and took an active part in handling the affairs of state with her husband. When Otto died, their son, Otto II, became king.

Bad news! Otto II's wife, Theophano, was jealous of Adelaide and was NOT nice to her. Then Otto II died, and his infant son, Otto III, became king and Theophano became "regent" (the one who would rule until the infant king grew up). Once in charge, Theophano had Adelaide thrown out of the court!

BUT in a few years, Theophano also died. And Adelaide returned to the court as regent for her grandson—and again was a prudent and understanding ruler of the kingdom.

In the midst of this topsy-turvy life, Adelaide was always a holy, prayerful woman, who helped the poor and built many churches and monasteries. She turned the bad news into good news and became a saint!

A lot of people seem to lead "good news-bad news" lives. Some of them concentrate ONLY on the BAD news! They look and act miserable and are always complaining and making excuses for themselves. Others focus on the GOOD news, smile, make the BEST of each day, "turn lemons into lemon meringue pie," and have a happy life. Which kind of person will YOU be?

Albert the Great

SOME people thought this saint had "magical powers"! Actually, he was an expert SCIENTIST—but most people didn't know about such things in his day, so they thought he must be MAGIC!

He was an authority on physics, geography, astronomy, mineralogy, biology, AND philosophy—and he taught and wrote about ALL those subjects. But his most IMPORTANT work was APPLYING his knowledge on those subjects to teaching and writing about GOD!

Albert was a bishop, a defender of the Faith, an adviser to a pope, a preacher, a teacher, a leader. He was NOT magic, but he WAS a GREAT and good man.

Would YOU like to be a scientist? ALL of the subjects Albert studied and taught were fascinating in and of themselves, BUT Albert realized that God was—and is—in EACH of them. All the mysteries of the universe were created by God. All knowledge comes from him. So no matter WHICH subjects you choose to study, the MOST fascinating subject to study will always be God!

Alexander, the Charcoal-Burner

This saint became a bishop because the people who lived in his town were snooty and sarcastic!

Alexander's town needed a new bishop. So the people in charge of finding one selected some "candidates" and then sent for another bishop—a wise man known as Gregory the Wonder-Worker—to come and decide which one would be right for the job.

Gregory came and talked to all the candidates, but NONE of them seemed to be the RIGHT one. The townspeople wanted him to choose someone rich and influential, but Gregory reminded them that Jesus' apostles had been poor, ordinary men.

So one of the townspeople said sarcastically, "Well, then, why don't you just pick Alexander, the Charcoal-Burner!" Gregory KNEW this was a smart-alecky suggestion, but he surprised them all by SENDING for Alexander!

When Alexander arrived, his clothes were all dirty and ragged because of the work he did, and he certainly didn't LOOK like a bishop. But when Gregory began to talk to him, he found out that Alexander was well educated and a very wise man. He learned that Alexander had given away all his money and taken a lowly job so he could live a simple life like Jesus.

Gregory knew he had found the RIGHT man to be bishop. What began as a JOKE ended JOYFULLY! The Charcoal-Burner became a good and holy bishop, a helpful teacher—and a saint!

Does your family or anyone in your neighborhood use a charcoal burner to barbecue? The next time you smell or eat a charcoaled hamburger, think of Alexander—the saint who CHOSE to take a lowly job but was then CHOSEN to be a great leader.

Aloysius

This saint planned to be a soldier HERO—UNTIL he read some books and became a different KIND of hero!

Aloysius' father was a marquis who was in the service of the king of Spain, and he wanted his son to be a great soldier. But when Aloysius was about twelve years old, he got very sick and had to rest and be quiet. This was no time to play soldier, so he read books. (There was NO TV back then!)

So what kind of books do you think he read? He read about the lives of the saints! Wouldn't he have been surprised to know that some day HE would be included in books about saints, and YOU would be reading about HIM?

Aloysius also read stories about Jesuit priests who had gone off to India to be missionaries—and that sounded pretty heroic to him. So Aloysius decided he wanted to be a priest instead of a soldier—and that's what he did. He became a heroic priest AND a saint.

> Do you think anyone will ever read about YOU in a book? If not in a saint book, in ANY kind of book? Well, don't be so sure! Aloysius didn't think so either! Reading can open all kinds of "doors" for you—giving you new ideas, new directions, new possibilities. Why don't you start today to read at least PART of a book EVERY day? It will be fun— AND something you read just might trigger a plan that will make YOU a hero some day!

Alphonsus Liguori

You might call this saint a "legal eagle"! It was reported that in eight years of practicing law, he NEVER lost a case!

During those years, Alphonsus enjoyed "society life" and "fashionable amusements" and began to neglect his religion. But one year during Lent, he made a retreat and gave some serious thought to what direction his life should take. Alphonsus decided he would NOT MARRY (although his father kept trying to "arrange" a marriage for him), and he would continue practicing law until something happened to show him God wanted him NOT to be a lawyer. Just a few months later, something DID happen!

During a court case, Alphonsus made a long, impassioned speech and was sure he had impressed everyone enough so that his client was sure to win. But then the opposing attorney handed Alphonsus a document with a marked passage and said, "You just wasted your breath! You disregarded the evidence on which the whole case depends." Alphonsus had read the document before but had MISSED the important part. He couldn't believe he could have done something so stupid! Because of his mistake, this important case was lost. Alphonsus left the court and never went back.

He felt this was a sign that God wanted him to leave the law and do something new. And he did. Alphonsus not only became a priest, he also became famous for his many writings on religious subjects, and then he founded a whole NEW Order of priests—the Redemptorists. Today, Redemptorists all over the world write, preach, and do missionary work—following the example of this "legal eagle" who God sent flying in a new direction.

> Would you like to be a lawyer some day? Or would you rather be an eagle? Well, you probably won't sprout wings but you COULD be a pilot or work for an airline or just take a trip on an airplane! Then you could look out the window of the plane and marvel at how God made the clouds and skies and birds—and YOU! You know, YOU are the most amazing example of God's creation! Of all the creatures God made, only people have the ability to think and choose and help and love and laugh! Use your brain right now to think of some OTHER things God made. Let's see. Aardvarks and arctic snow, dinosaurs and dandelions, tomatoes and tomcats, potatoes and planets, zebras and zircon, and zillions of other things! Why don't you see how LONG a list you can make, listing things God made! And don't forget to put YOUR NAME at the top of the list!

Anne and Joachim

These two people might be called Saints Grandma and Grandpa! Why? Because they were Jesus' grandparents!

Anne and Joachim were married for a long time but had NO children. They were good and holy people and wanted very much to have a baby of their own, so they prayed every day that God would send them a child. Finally, their prayers were answered, and they had a beautiful baby girl and named her Mary.

When Mary grew up, she became the mother of Jesus—and that made Anne and Joachim his grandma and grandpa!

There were no newspapers, books, or TV programs when they lived, so the only way "news" was spread was by word of mouth—somebody telling somebody who in turn told somebody else! Since nothing was written down, we don't know much about their lives—whether they lived near Mary and helped take care of Jesus or whether he visited with them and "slept over." We don't know if Anne baked cookies for him or if Joachim took him fishing. We DO know they were GOOD people, so they must have also been GOOD grandparents!

Grandpas and grandmas can be a lot of FUN! Too bad that today a lot of them live in different towns and seldom get to see their grandchildren. If YOU have grandparents far away, why don't you surprise them by writing a letter or sending them a card today! If you have grandparents nearby, call and suggest you DO something together soon. OR maybe you could just say a prayer today for ALL grandparents, asking God to bless them and make them happy!

Ansgar

If you could ask God for ONE favor, what would it be—lots of money, a fancy car, a new house? Ansgar asked for something very different. This saint once said that if he could ask God for one miracle, he would ask that God make him a good man!

Evidently, God DID do that without Ansgar having to ask for the miracle. When he was just a teenager, Ansgar began to teach young children in an abbey school in Germany. Later, he was sent to Sweden as a missionary and on the way, his ship was attacked by pirates, who seized everything.

His life was a series of triumphs and failures. He became an archbishop in Germany and organized missions in Denmark, Norway, and Sweden. But a great invasion of Vikings destroyed his city in Germany, and his missionaries were run out of Sweden.

After each disaster, Ansgar worked again to bring God's teachings to the people. He was very kind to the poor, and even washed their feet and waited on tables to serve them food. No matter how difficult things became, Ansgar did not get discouraged or give up. He continued to be a "good man."

> YOU probably will never have to worry about attacks by pirates or invasions of Vikings, but if you ever get discouraged OR if you ever get a chance to make ONE magical wish, think about Ansgar's wish. Would YOU ever wish for that?

Anthony of Padua

Quick now! Can you remember all the states in the United States, which year the American Civil War began, or how many miles there are between New York and San Francisco? Well, maybe you need Saint Anthony to help you!

Saint Anthony was known to have a marvelous memory! When he was very young, he began to study the Bible, and because of his retentive memory (which helped him retain or hang onto everything he learned), he gained a great knowledge of the Scriptures.

Anthony wanted to be a missionary, so he left his home in Portugal to go to Morocco, but he got very sick and had to head back home. On the way home, his ship got blown off course, and Anthony ended up in Italy instead of Portugal! One day while he was there, he went to a big gathering of Dominican and Franciscan priests. Someone was supposed to preach, but there had been a mix-up and no one came PREPARED for the occasion. So Anthony was asked if he would just get up and say whatever the Holy Spirit put into his mind!

Anthony did as he was asked and began very slowly, but once he got going, he gave such a wonderful talk that everyone knew he should become a preacher. And that's what he did! His great memory helped him recall what he was supposed to say, and he had a rich, strong voice that could carry a long way—an important thing in those days when microphones had not yet been invented!

Wherever Anthony spoke, crowds came to listen, and he convinced many people to become Christians. Because of his memory, his long hours of studying, and a ship blown off course, Anthony found his lifework preaching in Italy and spent his last years there in the town called Padua.

> Is it easy for you to remember what you have read, to memorize dates and facts, to hear a story and be able to tell someone else that same story exactly the way you heard it? Or is that hard for you? Some people just naturally remember things, and others have to work harder to memorize. Some people know exactly what they want to do as a career and DO IT, but others start out in one direction and then their ship gets blown in a NEW direction! One is not better than the other—just different. Be grateful for whatever YOUR special talents are and say a prayer today to ask God to blow you in whatever direction he wants you to travel!

Apollinaris the Apologist

When Apollinaris made an "apology," he didn't say he was sorry for something, he said he was PROUD of it! And what was he proud of? His Christian faith!

You see, the word *apology* has two very different meanings. When you do something wrong or impolite or improper, you usually say "Oh, I'm sorry" to apologize for your actions. BUT when you are making a scholarly defense of an idea or a belief, THAT is also called an "apology." If a scientist has a theory, he might make an apology for it to try to prove his idea and convince others of its

worth. In the same way, Saint Apollinaris made an apology to the emperor of his day, defending the Christian religion.

Apollinaris was evidently VERY convincing because the emperor then issued an edict forbidding anyone to denounce a Christian because of his or her religion—AND Apollinaris became known as The Apologist!

> Did YOU ever make an apology to say you're sorry for something? Most people have done that! But ONE thing you will never have to say you're sorry for is your Christian religion! If you ever make an apology for that, it can be the kind of apology that DEFENDS your faith and says you're PROUD to be a friend of Jesus.

Athanasius

This saint began his clerical life as a SECRETARY—the secretary to the Bishop of Alexandria. Later, Athanasius became a bishop himself, but a great heresy called Arianism began to

spread in the Mediterranean world, and Athanasius spent many difficult years struggling to defend the basic teachings of the Church.

His enemies tried to get rid of him by accusing him falsely of various crimes, but he was found innocent. They even tried to accuse him of murdering a man everyone knew was ALIVE and in hiding! Athanasius was always being banished or attacked or having to flee the city. He spent SEVENTEEN years in-and-out of exile! But Athanasius never gave up, and he never gave IN to those who attacked the Church.

The old proverb "Athanasius Against the World" arose because he became known as a man who was not afraid to face a whole world of enemies, defending what he KNEW was right!

Do you ever feel that YOU are alone against the world? You never have to feel you are ALONE if you are working for what is right—because then God is with you. If you ever have to fight long and hard against something you KNOW is wrong, remember Athanasius—who never gave up and never gave in!

Augustine

Did you ever see a hippo at the zoo? Well, this saint was the bishop of a town named HIPPO! As you know, a hippopotamus is one of the biggest animals in the zoo, and Augustine is one of the biggest saints in the Church—NOT because of his size but because of all the things he did!

Augustine's mother was a holy woman who taught him about Christianity when he was a youngster, but when he grew up and left home, Augustine FORGOT all his mother's teachings and lived a wild and crazy life.

Augustine's mother kept praying for him. Finally, he saw what a mistake he had made and returned to the Church and became one of the most famous Church leaders in history.

He was such a great writer that his books are still studied TODAY, hundreds of years after his death. During his life, Augustine wrote TWO HUNDRED treatises (explanations of Church principles and teachings), THREE HUNDRED letters of instruction, and almost FOUR HUNDRED sermons—PLUS his books!

In spite of a bad beginning, Augustine turned his life around and gave it a spectacular ending!

Did you ever make a mistake and think you could EVER make up for doing such a dumb thing? Well, you know, no matter what you do, God will ALWAYS forgive you if you are truly sorry and tell him so. No matter what bad mistake you make, you can always CHANGE and do better next time. So if you ever get discouraged because of something dumb you did, say you're sorry and resolve to NEVER do that again. Then ask God to help you turn yourself around— just like Saint Augustine did.

Bartholomea Capitanio

Would you believe that this lady became famous because she wrote so many letters? Well, that was ONE of the reasons!

When Bartholomea was a little girl, her father drank too much and made life very difficult for her and her mother. They both loved HIM but HATED his drinking. They tried to be patient and prayed for him.

When Bartholomea was a teenager, she noticed that many of the children in her town just "hung out" in the streets because there were no schools for them. So Bartholomea studied and got a teacher's certificate and opened a school in her home. In the evenings she began writing letters to friends and former students. Her letters offered spiritual counsel, advice, and friendship. People

SAVED her letters and "treasured" them. They often shared them with others, and priests even made copies of the letters to give to people who came to them for advice.

Although she died when she was only twenty-six years old, Saint Bartholomea had already written A LOT. THREE HUNDRED of her letters were collected and published and are still read today.

Many people have relatives or friends who drink too much like Bartholomea's father did, but TODAY there are treatment centers to help them. If you know anyone like that, pray for him or her to get help. Maybe you could even write that person a letter! Do you LIKE to write letters? Not many people WRITE letters today, but it's always great to GET a letter! Why don't you write a letter to SOMEONE today? Who will that someone be?

Basil

Here's a saint who was not afraid to fuss at an emperor! Basil lashed out at his emperor, telling the emperor he had been cruel to his people and he did not live by proper Christian principles. The emperor was NOT pleased and said, "No one has ever spoken to me like that!" Basil shot right back, "Then apparently you have never met a Catholic bishop before!"

Basil was a GREAT bishop who lived in what would seem to you a strange and exotic civilization—the Byzantine Empire. His was the FIRST Christian nation, and many of the great events of the early Church came from there—the first Church councils, the first great teachers of the Church, and some of the first worst problems, too. This was a world where the Church was in great danger of being crushed by its enemies, but brave Basil and other courageous Church leaders defended the Faith and saved the Church!

Would YOU have the nerve to speak up to an emperor and tell him he was not living a Christian life? Not many people would have such courage. Not many people could be as brave as the saints of the early Church. You will probably never NEED to speak to an emperor, but you DO NEED to be brave in YOUR world today—to say NO to people who want you to get involved with drugs or alcohol or an immoral lifestyle. Say a prayer today that God will give you courage to lead a good life and to SPEAK UP when it's important—just like Saint Basil did!

Bathildis

This saint had a real Cinderella story! She was a slave who became a queen and the mother of three kings!

Bathildis was born in Britain but was sold as a slave to the mayor of the court of the king of France. She was evidently very capable and charming and made quite an impression at court because the king married her! She went from being a servant to being a queen!

She and her husband had three sons. When her husband died, Bathildis reigned as the ruler of the kingdom. She was a wise and just ruler, did many good things for her people, and ransomed many who were slaves like she had been. She was queen for seven years until her oldest son became old enough to be crowned king. Later, her two other sons also wore the crown.

After her sons were enthroned, Bathildis left the palace and its royal trappings to go to a humble convent. There she became a nun and asked to be given the lowliest jobs. She went from slave to queen to servant of God.

Do you like to read Cinderella stories, rags-to-riches tales of people who go from poor to rich, low to high? Why don't you write your OWN Cinderella story today? Think about where you are and what you are doing NOW—and what you would LIKE to do or be SOME DAY? Would you like to be rich or famous or athletic or well educated or have a big family or drive a big car or take a trip around the world or travel through space? Or would you like to discover a cure for the common cold, a new planet, a new ice-cream flavor? Or would you like to make the world better by being a good person, a good friend, a good Christian?

Bede the Venerable

Here's a man who had a special name! He was not just called Bede—but Venerable Bede! Now, how do you guess that happened?

Well, not only was Bede the most learned man of his time, he was so wise in the ways of the Lord that people thought of him as venerable—one to be treated with reverence, respect, and admiration.

And what a writer he was! Bede wrote about history, rhetoric, cosmography, orthography, astronomy, music, grammar,

philosophy, poetry, exegesis, and hagiography. Do you think maybe he might also be called Venerable Jack-of-All-Trades?

Most people of Bede's day didn't even know enough about ONE subject to write a book about it. And they probably didn't even know WHAT some of Bede's subjects were—like orthography, exegesis, or hagiography. Do YOU know what those things are? Why don't you get out the dictionary and look up some of the things Bede wrote about? And then maybe YOU would like to write a book—or a report or a letter to someone—about one of those subjects!

Benedict

Do you have a sister? Or a best friend or relative you love and ALSO like a lot? Well, what if you could see that person only ONE DAY each year? That's the way it was with Benedict and his sister Scholastica!

Benedict founded the Benedictine Order of monks way back in the fifth century, and he made an important difference to the world of the Middle Ages. Thousands of men entered monasteries to follow Benedict's motto for life: "Pray and work." Benedictines brought Christianity to many countries that had never heard of Jesus, AND they worked to RENEW an interest in religion, education, and culture in countries where the Faith had been dying. They also helped build many of the great cathedrals in Europe.

You can see that Benedict was a very great man—and his sister was a great lady. (See page 128 to learn more about Scholastica.) Although Scholastica lived only a few miles from Benedict, they would only allow themselves to meet once a year! They would have lunch together and spend the whole day talking—and do you know what they talked about? Well, they probably shared news of what each had been doing that year, BUT since they were both very religious, they spent a good part of their day talking about God and his Church and religion and such things as the joys of heaven!

> If you could spend only one day a year visiting your sister or your favorite person, what would YOU talk about? Would you spend ANY of that time talking about God? Well, maybe you should! Maybe you should spend SOME time EVERY day talking about God! What could be a more mysterious and intriguing subject!

Benedict Joseph Labre

If you had seen this saint on the street, you might have NOT wanted to associate with him! He was a wanderer who sometimes wore ragged clothes and looked like a tramp.

This Benedict was the oldest son in a family of EIGHTEEN children! His uncle, who was a parish priest, taught Benedict his school lessons. But when Benedict was old enough, he began to wander. After traveling from monastery to monastery, he decided to become a pilgrim, going from one shrine to the next. Finally, Benedict came to Rome, and for a while he even slept in the Colosseum and became known as the "Beggar of Rome."

To many, Benedict must have seemed like a failure, but he was seeking God. He was so focused on God that he didn't think it was important to bother about nice clothes or a fancy place to stay. He impressed all who knew him with his devotion to the Blessed Sacrament and with his deep spirituality. He was an example of how little the opinion of the world matters when you are seeking to please God alone.

Everyone "wanders" sometime—restless, searching, wondering what to do next, where to go, what book to read, what movie to see, what friend to call, what clothes to wear. But these are worldly wanderings. Do you ever "wander" to church to make a little secret visit or wander to a quiet place to pray the rosary or wander outside to take a walk and talk to God? Maybe you should try it sometime—like maybe today?

Bénezet

This saint was a shepherd who built a bridge—and became known as Bénezet the Bridge Builder. One day Bénezet had a dream or vision in which he was told he should build a bridge at a certain spot over the Rhone River, because many travelers had lost their lives trying to cross there. Building a bridge was NOT exactly what a shepherd would usually do! But Bénezet must have believed strongly that this was what God WANTED him to do, so he went to the local bishop and told him about his dream and asked for help. Amazingly, the bishop gave his approval for this gigantic task.

For the next seven years, Bénezet worked on this project, and with God's help, was able to get all the materials necessary and solve all the engineering problems involved in building a stone bridge across a large river. Bénezet died before the bridge was completed; but during the time he worked on it, many miracles had been reported as a result of the prayers of this shepherd-bridge-builder. After Bénezet died, the people of the town honored him as a saint and finished building his bridge!

Can you imagine starting a project as big as building a bridge, with no money and no experience? Many of the saints were able to accomplish stupendous feats that SEEMED impossible—not because of their own ability but because they put their faith and trust in God and firmly believed he would be at their side to help them. If you ever have a job that seems IMPOSSIBLE, remember the shepherd who built a bridge; then ask God to help YOU too!

Benilde

Do you know what the "daily grind" is? It's those humdrum ordinary things most people have to do every day—same old, same old. Well, Pope Pius XI called Benilde the "saint of the daily grind."

As a young boy, this saint went to a school run by the Christian Brothers in France. But when he graduated, instead of leaving, he stayed! Benilde became a Christian Brother himself and spent the rest of his life TEACHING young boys.

The "daily grind" usually means doing the same job over and over, day after day, and Benilde did that all his life—BUT teaching is never REALLY same old, same old, because there is ALWAYS something NEW to learn and then to teach. And that's what Benilde did!

He was the principal of one school for a few years, and then he started a new one. It became known as a model school, and Benilde became known as a model teacher AND a model Christian.

Do YOU ever get tired of doing the same old things every day—get out of bed, wash your face, brush your teeth, eat breakfast, go to school, do work after school, eat supper, go to bed? Those are all good and necessary things to do, but why don't you do something EXTRA today? Pretend YOU are a teacher, and think what you would say and do to TEACH somebody something—how to tie a shoe, throw a ball, bake a cake, sew on a button, write a story, sing a song, say a prayer! Do you think you would be a GOOD teacher?

Bernadette

This saint NEVER DID make good grades in school! But she DID change the mind of a bishop—AND the world!

Bernadette was a poor girl who just couldn't seem to learn her lessons—even when someone tried to "tutor" her, one-on-one. Her father was a miller, but the family had very little money and lived in a small place almost as damp as a cave. This was not healthy for Bernadette, who had asthma and was often very sick.

One day, Bernadette was gathering firewood on a riverbank and suddenly saw a bright light and a beautiful lady. It was Mary, the Blessed Mother. Bernadette felt so happy, but she was also very frightened. She ran home and told her mother and her friends what she had seen, but no one believed her.

Bernadette went back to the riverbank, and the "beautiful lady" came to visit her again and again. The Blessed Mother told Bernadette to dig in the ground, and a trickle of water came out and then a SPRING of fresh, gurgling water. Some of the people in the town heard what was happening, and a

mother whose baby was dying, bathed her baby in the spring and the baby got well!

Soon crowds of people began to gather to watch Bernadette pray the rosary and then talk to the "beautiful lady" only SHE could see. The parish priest didn't believe her. The bishop didn't believe her. And the police were MAD at her for causing crowds to gather.

But the Blessed Mother gave a special message to Bernadette to take to the bishop. Then HE believed Bernadette, and soon EVERYONE believed her. The Blessed Mother also asked for a church to be built on the spot where she had appeared, and today a beautiful basilica is there—and MANY MIRACLES have occurred when people came to pray.

After the "officials" finally believed Bernadette and they began to build the church, she left her home to become a nun and to spend the rest of her life working and praying in the convent.

Since then, MILLIONS of people have come to see the town of Lourdes, France, where a little girl who made bad grades in school was visited by the Blessed Mother. This shrine has become one of the most popular in the whole world. It is nestled in the Pyrenees Mountains and is known as the shrine of Our Lady of Lourdes.

> Did YOU ever make bad grades in school? It takes hard work to make good grades, but SOME people can work hard and STILL not make the grade! It's harder for them to learn—just as it was hard for Bernadette. But Bernadette DID learn the most IMPORTANT lesson—how to pray and how to love God with all her heart. It doesn't take a genius to do that! Have YOU learned that lesson?

Bernardino Tomitani

When Bernardino stood up to preach his first homily, guess what happened? He got so SCARED, he forgot what he was going to say!

Bernardino always loved to read and study. His mother sometimes had to MAKE him close his books and go outside to play. When he grew up, he became a priest and studied philosophy and law and ENJOYED his studies. But THEN his superior told him he must start preaching. Bernardino was AFRAID to stand up and speak in public. He was more comfortable with his books than with people! But he had to do what he was told to do.

He had chosen the name Bernardino in honor of Saint Bernardino of Siena. On that saint's feast day, THIS Bernardino was sent to preach in a large church. When he stood up to talk, he was so nervous, he forgot the whole homily he had carefully prepared! BUT the people were waiting to hear SOMETHING, so he began to tell about the saint whose name he had chosen. He KNEW a lot about this saint and just began to talk from his heart—and soon FORGOT to be afraid.

The people were so touched by his talk that he was asked to preach more and more. Bernardino began to preach against selfishness and greed, and the people listened. As a result, he was even able to get some LAWS changed to protect people's rights. Wherever he went, huge crowds came to hear Blessed Bernardino, and soon the man who had been AFRAID TO SPEAK in public became the most popular preacher in all of Italy!

Have YOU ever been afraid to stand up and speak in public? When you have to make a report or even answer a question, do you get so scared, your knees shake, and your voice trembles? If that ever happens to you, try practicing in front of a mirror. Try praying for courage. Try remembering Blessed Bernardino. And who knows—maybe you, too, will some day become a FAMOUS speaker.

Bertilla Boscardin

Can you imagine what it would be like nursing wounded soldiers in a hospital on the front lines of a battle in the middle of an air raid? That's what Sister Bertilla did.

This nun was known as Annetta "the goose" when she was a little girl because others thought she was too dumb to learn much or do much. She was from a poor family and had little education, having to work as a servant to help support her family. She did simple tasks like washing dishes, doing laundry, cleaning houses—and everyone thought that's all she could ever do.

When she was sixteen, Annetta joined the convent and became Sister Bertilla. She told the other Sisters that she didn't know how to do much, but she wanted to learn and she wanted to become a saint!

Her superior decided that Sister Bertilla just might make a good nurse, and THIS changed her life. She seemed to have a real TALENT for nursing and became a much-loved, efficient, caring nurse in the children's ward of a hospital in Italy. THEN, in 1915, during the First World War, the Italian army took over the hospital and used it to care for wounded soldiers. ALL those in the hospital—both nurses and wounded—were terrified by the air raids, but Sister Bertilla stayed and cared for those who were too sick to be moved to a safer place.

After the war was over, the children's ward reopened,

and Sister Bertilla was able to nurse the little ones again—without worrying about air raids. In her life, "the goose" achieved both of her wishes—she learned and she became a saint!

> Would you like to work in a hospital? Would you like to be in an air raid? Would you like to be a saint? Well, maybe you won't ever do ANY of these things, but you COULD do something Sister Bertilla did. She said she wanted to LEARN, and you can always do that. Instead of being a "goose," learn something NEW today—and every day!

Bonaventure

Here's a saint who might have had "dishpan hands"! But if he did, he could have kept the secret "under his hat"!

When the pope decided to make Bonaventure a cardinal, he sent a delegation to announce the news and to present him with the official red cardinal hat. But when they got to his monastery, they found Bonaventure washing dishes! And he told them to just hang his new hat on a tree until he finished!

Bonaventure must have been a very humble man—but he was

39

also a very learned one. He was known to have one of the great minds of medieval times and was an outstanding theologian, philosopher, writer, and preacher. He wrote and spoke so beautifully about heavenly things, he became known as the "Seraphic (angelic) Doctor." But he was down-to-earth enough to help with the chores!

Most famous people wouldn't spend their time doing something as "lowly" as washing dishes! But most saints WOULD! Do YOU ever wash dishes? Or stack dishes in the dishwasher? Why don't you help out the family and do that TODAY! And while you're working with the dishes, think of this humble saint and "tip your hat" to Saint Bonaventure!

Boniface IV (Pope)

This saint's name sounds like "bonny"—or happy—face! And he had good reason to HAVE a happy face, because he accomplished something very unusual.

When Boniface became pope, there was a large ROUND building in Rome known as the Pantheon. It had been a "temple of all gods" where the Romans worshiped false gods. So Boniface decided to "rehabilitate" it and turn it into a Christian church to honor the TRUE God. And then the "new" church got a new—and unusual—name. Because of its round shape, it became known as "Santa Maria Rotunda."

Have you ever been in a round building? Would you like to live in one? If you did, you would be "going around in circles" ALL DAY! Instead of going around in circles today, think about how God is like a circle—no beginning, no ending, is, always was, always will be. Isn't that a "bonny thought"?

Bridget of Sweden

Gulp!

Bridget was said to have one foot in heaven and the other firmly planted on earth! Although she was a good and "saintly" person, she was also a busy, down-to-earth kind of lady.

Bridget's mother was a cousin of the king of Sweden. Her father was governor of Upland and the richest man in the country. When Bridget married, trumpets sounded, and the celebration lasted for three days—with dancing, music, and feasting for everyone (including all the poor of the town)!

Bridget and her husband had eight children and a very busy happy family life—but Bridget still found time for prayer and good works. One of her daughters later said, "Mother helped all who had a hard life—whether they were poor, sinners, pilgrims, orphans, or widows. To all of them, she was the most gentle, most compassionate mother."

In spite of her gentleness, Bridget did NOT hesitate to speak up when she saw a problem. When she was called to the royal court to help educate the king's new bride, she was shocked to find the court's lifestyle NOT very Christian. She loudly criticized the king, the queen, the clergy, and the members of the court, who were either immoral or lacking in virtue and charity. She even told the king he was acting like a "disobedient, naughty child." Although Bridget was right, some members of the court got very angry and were glad when she left.

Years later, after her husband died and her children were grown, Bridget gave all her rich possessions to her children or to the poor and went to live in a monastery. When she felt God wanted her to "hit the road," she traveled from Sweden to Rome—a journey that took eight months—and then to Jerusalem. And wherever she went, Bridget tried to help those who needed help and did not hesitate to criticize those who NEEDED to be criticized.

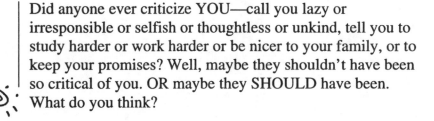

Did anyone ever criticize YOU—call you lazy or irresponsible or selfish or thoughtless or unkind, tell you to study harder or work harder or be nicer to your family, or to keep your promises? Well, maybe they shouldn't have been so critical of you. OR maybe they SHOULD have been. What do you think?

Brigid (Bride)

Did you know there was a saint named Bride? Well, that was her nickname, but her real name was Brigid.

She was a very famous lady in Ireland and founded a monastery that became a center of learning and spirituality. She also founded a school of art where they made illustrated "illuminated" manuscripts that became famous. It is said that this "Bride" was patient, prayerful, firm, faithful, forgiving, and helpful to anyone in trouble. In spite of her many achievements, it is also said that she BLUSHED every time she spoke.

Did you ever blush or know someone who blushed—turned red in the face at the most embarrassing times? Today would be a good time to fix yourself a Strawberry Blush. Just mix some milk with mashed-up fresh or frozen strawberries and add some sugar if you like. As you sip your Blush, remember Saint "Bride" and think what you could do to become patient, prayerful, firm, faithful, forgiving, and helpful to anyone in trouble. And if you think you could never be ALL those things, at least you could try to be SOME of them!

Cajetan

You might call this saint the "Loan arRanger"! Or maybe not. You might even call him the first one to run a pawn shop. Or at least the first one to start a credit union.

Cajetan accomplished a great many things in his life. Of noble parentage, he received university degrees in both canon and civil

He's the Loan Arranger.

law. He was a senator and was appointed to a lofty position by the pope. But he chose to leave all this to work with the poor and sick in Rome, going through the streets and into the shacks, seeking out those who needed help. His friends were shocked that he would do such "dirty" work, but Cajetan wanted to serve others.

When he saw that moneylenders were taking advantage of poor people by charging them huge interest rates, Cajetan decided to put a stop to that. He began a business that would make loans to poor people and charge them fair interest rates. It could be compared to today's credit unions, where employees can make low-cost loans, OR to pawn shops, where people can take something they own and get a loan on it until they can afford to "buy it back."

Since the poor often have times when they desperately need to make a loan to get by for a while, the people were very grateful to Cajetan for arranging it so they could make a loan without being cheated. And that's why you COULD call Cajetan the Loan Arranger!

Did you ever watch any old movies about the Lone Ranger—a man who wore a mask and rode a white horse and helped people in trouble? Well—except for the mask—he sounds a bit like Saint Cajetan! The ones who SHOULD have worn the mask were the moneylenders, who were cheating the poor people! Do YOU ever feel so ashamed of something you have done that you feel like you should hide behind a mask? If that ever happens, make a confession right away. After you say you're sorry and receive the sacrament of penance, you can promise to never do something so bad again—so you'll never have to feel so bad again!

Catherine of Siena

This saint was the youngest in a family of twenty-five children! She was a merry, happy little girl who grew up to be the most remarkable woman of her time.

Because of her advice and counseling, many people changed their lives and returned to the Church. Because of her ability to "heal" feuds, many people came to her to help settle disagreements.

Because of her wisdom, she became a great influence on those who read her writing. Because of her goodness, she even became a counselor to the pope! And because of her love for God, she became a saint.

Do YOU come from a large family like Saint Catherine or from a small family? Very FEW people come from a family as large as Saint Catherine's, but SIZE is not what makes a happy family. What do YOU think it takes to make a happy family? What could you do TODAY to make someone happy in your family?

Clare of Assisi

This saint scared off a whole army! So how do you think she did it?

Clare was born in the little town of Assisi—the same town where Saint Francis was born. She became a nun and founded the Poor Clares. She and all the Sisters wanted to live like the poor, so theirs was a very simple, frugal life. When Clare's father died and left her a fortune, she gave it all away to the poor.

One day, an enemy army invaded the valley where her convent was located and began devastating the countryside. The soldiers put a ladder against the wall of the convent intending to come in through the window! But Clare got a monstrance (a receptacle in which the consecrated host is exposed for adoration) and held it up to the window while she and the other Sisters prayed. When the soldiers saw the monstrance with the Blessed Sacrament, they were suddenly filled with fear and ran away in terror. The convent was saved.

Saint Clare didn't use a gun or a knife to fight the enemy. She used faith and prayer. Today, too many people think they have to own dangerous weapons and USE them. They have forgotten the words from the Bible: "Love your neighbor as yourself." Will YOU ever forget those words?

Cloud of Metz

Saint CLOUD? Rain Cloud, Fleecy Cloud, Cumulus Cloud, Thunder Cloud, yes—but SAINT Cloud? Yes!

Also known as Cloudulf, this saint lived way back in the seventh century in a town that was part of the holy Roman Empire. He was a devout layman, then a model pastor, AND the Bishop of Metz for over forty years.

Now today, hundreds of years later, there is a place in the United States that has HIS NAME— Saint Cloud, Minnesota!

Do you like cloudy days? Or do you like sunny ones better? Do you like cloudbursts, when the rain suddenly splish-splashes down in torrents, then just as suddenly stops? Or do you prefer nice, gentle, long-lasting showers? Whatever today is—rain or shine, splish-splash or pitter-pat—get out an atlas and an encyclopedia and look up Saint Cloud, Minnesota. See if you can find out WHY a city in twentieth-century United States has the same name as a saint from long, long ago.

Colette

This saint was christened Nicolette, but called Colette. And she was a traveler.

In her early twenties, Colette became a nun and was known for her deep spirituality. She planned to live a quiet life, but one day while praying, she changed her mind! She decided it was her "calling" to open new convents with stricter rules than some other convents had at that time.

Colette began to travel and journeyed through-out France and Flanders. In spite of many obstacles, she was able to open seventeen new convents and reform numerous other convents under the rule of the Poor Clares. One branch of this group was even named the Colettines.

This saint started out to keep her feet firmly planted in one spot, but then God gave her "travelin' shoes"!

Do YOU like to travel? Would you like to take a trip around the world? Well, how about a trip around your own city? Why don't you start a collection of clippings and information about ALL the places to see and things to do in the town where you live? (And don't forget to include some of the beautiful old churches and/or shrines!) THEN get your family to help you plan some family field trips!

Crispin and Crispinian

Did you ever know anyone who "moonlighted"? No, it doesn't mean sitting outside looking at the moonlight. Moonlighting is what you do when you have TWO jobs—one in the daytime and one at night, when there's moonlight! Well, these two saints had two jobs. In the daytime, they would teach and preach and convert many people to the Christian faith. Then, at night, they would work as shoemakers—making new shoes and repairing old ones.

No one knows why their mother named them ALMOST the same name, but she did—and BOTH names are now saintly!

Did you ever get a hole in the sole of your shoe or run down your heels so they look like they've been peeled? Well, maybe you don't need NEW shoes; you just need to get them repaired by a good shoemaker like Crispin or Crispinian. Would YOU like to be a shoemaker or a caretaker or a candlemaker or an undertaker? How about an overtaker? Make a list of all the jobs you might like to have and another list of all the jobs you would NOT like to have. Then say a prayer that God will help you study and work so that someday you will have the job that HE would like you to have!

Cyril and Methodius

Do you celebrate Saint Valentine Day on February 14? Well, you really SHOULD also be celebrating Saints Cyril and Methodius Day—because February 14 is THEIR feast day, a special day set aside by the Church to honor them!

These two saints were brothers and worked together to spread the teachings of the Church to the Slavic people. As a young man, Cyril studied at the university in Constantinople with a teacher known as Leo the Grammarian. Cyril was such a good student that he later earned his own nickname, Cyril the Philosopher. His brother, Methodius, was also a learned man and at one time was the governor of a Slavic colony.

In 862 an ambassador of the prince of Moravia came to Constantinople asking for missionaries who could come and teach his people in their own language. Because of their knowledge of the language and their personal holiness, Cyril and Methodius were chosen to go.

Legend says that Cyril and his followers probably were the ones who "invented" the Cyrillic characters—adapted from Greek letters—that have since been used to write the Russian, Serbian, and Bulgarian language. This is one reason these brothers are also known as the fathers of Slavonic literary culture.

The next time you send someone a valentine, maybe you should address it in Cyrillic letters! Well, that would be VERY hard to do if you don't know that language. Instead maybe you could just say a little prayer of thanksgiving for the many wise Church leaders in history—like the brothers Cyril and Methodius.

Dismas

Tick Tick

Dismas is a person who might be called the "last minute" saint! He was a thief who was saved at the very last minute!

The day Jesus was crucified, two thieves were also crucified, one on each side of Jesus. One of the men was NOT sorry for his life of crime, but the other was Dismas and he WAS sorry. As Dismas was dying, he asked Jesus if his sins could be forgiven. Jesus told him yes by saying, "This day you will be with me in Paradise."

Do YOU ever put off things until the "last minute"? Saying you're sorry should NOT be one of those things! Dismas had a good excuse because he probably had never been taught how to live a good life and certainly didn't know much about Jesus' teachings until the very last minutes of his life. People today don't have that excuse! They have the Bible, books, teachers, and all Christians to tell them about Jesus' way to lead a happy life. But just in case YOU ever wait and hesitate to be sorry for a sin, remember Saint Dismas—a good reminder that it is NEVER too late to say you're sorry.

Donatus

Have you ever heard about somebody being at the wrong place at the wrong time? Well, Donatus was at the right place at the right time!

Donatus was an Irish nobleman who had been on a trip to Italy and just happened to pass through the village of Fiesole at a time when the clergy and people were trying to choose a new bishop. Donatus went into the cathedral, and just as he entered, the church bells suddenly began to ring, and all the candles blazed forth with a bright light!

The people all looked around and saw this stranger and immediately decided this had been a sign from heaven that Donatus should be their new bishop! Donatus agreed and became a good bishop, a gifted preacher, a poet, and a saint.

> Of course, people are not usually chosen for jobs in such a strange way today. But God DOES still send signs and messages to his people. You just have to pay attention! In fact, God may be sending YOU a message right now! So stop, look, and listen. What do you think God is saying to you TODAY?

Eligius

This saint was a GOLDSMITH—a master at making ornate items from precious metals and jewels. And, he was an honest man! One day King Clotaire II sent Eligius some gold and jewels and told him to make a throne. Eligius saw he wouldn't need all the rich materials the king sent BUT instead of keeping the "extras," he made the king TWO thrones. The king was surprised and delighted. He was impressed with Eligius' artistry—AND ALSO his honesty.

After that, Eligius was welcomed as a member of the court and was much admired for his goldsmithing talent. But the honest goldsmith ALSO became known for his generosity in giving away so much of his OWN "gold" to his poorer countrymen.

One day a man asked for directions to the house where Eligius lived. He was told to go to a certain street and then to "just look for a crowd of poor people in front of a house"—and THAT would be the home of Eligius!

The king and his son, Dagobert, became good friends of Eligius and gave him land to build a monastery and a convent. While building, Eligius realized he had been given more land than he needed and went to the court to explain. Dagobert said, "Some of my officers do not scruple to rob me of whole estates; whereas Eligius is afraid of having ONE INCH of ground which is not his."

> Do you know anyone as honest as Eligius? He COULD have been PROUD and uppity because of his talent, his friendship with royalty, and his wealth. Instead, he was humble and honest. Make a list today of everyone you know OR KNOW ABOUT who is OR WAS humble and honest. Could you put YOUR name on that list?

Elizabeth of Hungary

This saint was the daughter of the king of Hungary and the day she was BORN, she was promised in marriage to the son of a nobleman. When she was only four years old, she was taken to her future father-in-law's castle so she could GROW UP with her future husband.

When Elizabeth was barely a teenager and her "intended," Louis, was twenty-one, they were married. By then, they were already good friends, so Louis KNEW that Elizabeth would spend a lot of her time praying and doing charitable works—and he never objected.

Their castle was built on a steep rock, and Elizabeth realized it would be difficult for people who needed help to climb all the way up, so she built a hospital at the FOOT of the rock! She went there regularly to help care for the sick. She often fed them herself, made their beds, or did whatever was needed. She also arranged for the poor to be given food at her gate, and every day NINE HUNDRED people came to be fed.

Elizabeth lived a saintly life as a wife, the mother of three children, and a woman who shared her wealth with others. She became the patron saint of Catholic Charities.

Do you ever share YOUR wealth with others? If you had only two nickels, would you give one nickel to someone else? Maybe if you had A LOT of money like Elizabeth, it would be easier to share than when you just have a little. BUT A LOT of people who have A LOT of money NEVER share. And some people who have only A LITTLE

money share all the time. Which kind of person will you be?

Emily de Rodat

This lady probably became a saint because she did some eavesdropping! (When you eavesdrop, you either accidentally or on purpose OVERHEAR what somebody is saying to somebody else but NOT to you!)

When she was a young girl, Emily took care of little children on the playground and helped to teach them about God before they made their first Communion. Then she decided that she would

Hmmm...

become a nun so she joined a convent. But Emily just didn't feel like that convent was the right place for her. So she left and joined a DIFFERENT convent. Again, she didn't feel like she fit in there. So she left and joined ANOTHER convent. But she left that one too.

Then one day Emily was visiting a friend when she OVERHEARD some women talking about how hard it was to find someone to teach their children because they were poor and had no money to pay a teacher and all the schools in their town were too expensive. All of a sudden, Emily knew what she should do!

She invited some of the poor children to come to her room, and she began to teach them. Later, she was able to rent a house and asked three of her friends to help her and she opened a FREE school for poor children. Soon she had eight teachers and ONE HUNDRED children at her school.

But that was just the beginning. She and her friends decided to form a NEW religious community and more and more women joined them and their work grew and grew—just because God had let Emily OVERHEAR someone's conversation!

Have you noticed how God sometimes works in very strange ways? Emily kept trying to find where she was supposed to go, joining different convents, and then God sent her in a whole new direction! Has that ever happened to YOU? Did you ever think you knew what you wanted to do but it just didn't work out? Maybe you tried out for a ball team but didn't make it. Or you started to take piano lessons and then quit. Or you wanted to go to one school but had to go to a different one. You THOUGHT you knew where you should go because you WANTED to do that but God sent you off in a whole new direction. Never get discouraged when things don't work out the way you WANT them to—it could just mean that God has some place better to send you because he can see around the corners of the future and you can't!

Ethelreda (Audrey)

Police reports often use three letters after the name of someone who has more than ONE name. The letters are AKA and stand for "Also Known As." Well, THIS saint is AKA AUDREY!

Saint Ethelreda/ Audrey was the daughter of a king, and hers was a very special family. In addition to THIS saint, there were FOUR other saints in the family! In a listing of saints, you'll find Ethelreda and ALSO her brother, Erconwald, and her three sisters—Ethelburga, Sexburga, and Withburga.

Evodius

I'm a christian!

This saint lived in the same century that Jesus did and is said to be the FIRST one to use the word *Christian* to describe someone who believes in the divinity and the teachings of Jesus Christ!

Evodius was also said to be one of the seventy disciples ordained by the apostles themselves. He became the Bishop of Antioch and was PROBABLY consecrated by Saint Peter.

Evodius was privileged to know the people who KNEW Jesus.

Would YOU have liked to have known Jesus when he was on earth? What would you have said to him? What would you have asked him? Would YOU have been one of the first "Christians"? Would you have believed in and followed all the teachings of Jesus and told other people how to BE "Christian"? Do you do that NOW?

Fiacre

This is the patron saint of cab drivers—even though there WERE NO cabs or taxis in his day, and he has nothing in common with cab drivers, since he always wanted to be ALONE!

Fiacre grew up in Ireland but when he decided he wanted to be a monk or hermit, he couldn't find a place where he could be as ALONE as he wanted to be! So he sailed across the English Channel to France. Then he went to the bishop and told him he was looking for a place where he could pray and work alone.

That bishop had a small house in the middle of a forest, which he offered to Fiacre, and according to a legend, he told him he could have as much land around the house as he could plow in ONE DAY.

Well, Fiacre was pretty smart. Instead of using a regular plow, he used his staff (a walking stick) to furrow the land and was able to cover much more territory than he could have with a heavy plow. At the end of the day, he had plowed a large area, and the bishop kept his word and gave all that land to Fiacre.

Fiacre was happy to have found such a private, quiet place. He went to work and cleared the trees from the land and then planted a garden by the side of his house. Next, he built a small chapel and happily settled down to pray.

BUT people soon heard about this holy hermit in the forest and how he grew all kinds of vegetables, flowers, and herbs for medicine. Soon Fiacre had just what he did NOT want—visitors! Now Fiacre was not only holy, he was also hospitable. And kind.

When he learned some of the people had come a long way and had no where to stay, Fiacre built a small house so the travelers could stay overnight. More and more people came—poor ones to beg for food or medicine, troubled ones to ask for advice and prayers. Eventually, a small village developed around his hermitage and was named Saint Fiacre-in-Seine-et-Marne.

So what about the cab drivers? Well, years after the hermit's death, a hotel in Paris was named Hotel de St. Fiacre, and the very FIRST taxis in Paris—which were horse-drawn coaches—usually parked by that hotel. Soon the Paris taxis became known as "fiacres," and this saint—who had just wanted to be alone—became the PATRON of cab drivers!

Did you ever ride in a taxi? Would you like to be a cab driver some day? Would you like to go to Paris some day? It can be fun to travel to other parts of the world and see new sights and meet new people. But it can ALSO be nice to sometimes be ALONE like Saint Fiacre. The next time you're alone, get out a world atlas and think about which foreign language you would like to learn. OR read more about the saints and decide which saint you would most want to be like!

Frances of Rome

Have you ever heard any of those silly mother-in-law jokes? Well, you might have heard some about this saint if you had lived in her town because her daughter-in-law did NOT like her at all!

Frances was a sweet lady, who took good care of her husband and children, and they all loved her very much. She also went EVERY day to the local hospital to help patients there and was very kind to her large household of servants. Then some enemies destroyed her

palacc. Her husband and oldest son had to flee for their lives, and Frances and the younger children lived in a corner of their ruined home for several years until her husband and son were able to return. That's when her son married a girl named Mobilia. It looked like life would be beautiful again.

BUT, unfortunately, Mobilia had a terrible temper and decided she did NOT like Frances. Mobilia complained constantly, threw tantrums, and even made fun of Frances in public. Then one day when Mobilia was right in the middle of one of her tantrums, she suddenly fell ill. Frances tenderly took care of her and nursed her back to health. After that, Mobilia saw how wrong she had been. She, too, began to love her saintly mother-in-law and then followed her example and helped in her work with the poor and the sick.

 Did you ever NOT like somebody? Did you ever complain about somebody? Did you ever throw a tantrum? Think about somebody you do NOT like—and then surprise yourself! Do something NICE for that person! Surpriiiiisssssseeeeee....

Frances Xavier Cabrini

Did you ever know anyone who was afraid to go swimming, afraid to get in a boat, afraid of water? Well, here's a saint who was!

When Frances Cabrini was a little girl in Italy, she fell into a river. Although she was saved quickly, this was a terrifying experience for her; after that, she was always afraid of water. But when she grew up to do God's work, she had to cross NOT just a river but an OCEAN!

Frances always wanted to be a nun and go to work in the foreign missions, but there were no orders of missionary sisters, so she founded an order herself! It was called the Missionary Sisters of the Sacred Heart, and they worked to give Christian education for young girls. Then one day the pope told Frances that she should take some of the Sisters and go to work across the ocean in America!

After that first long voyage by sea, Frances—in spite of her fear of water—found herself traveling back and forth across the ocean many times, opening orphanages, hospitals, and schools in both America and Italy. Within a few years, her first group of eight Sisters grew to over a thousand nuns working in eight different countries. Pretty good for a little girl who was afraid of water!

Are you afraid of water? What ARE you afraid of? Does that fear STOP you from doing things you want to do or SHOULD do? Ask God today to help you forget fear and welcome adventure—like Saint Frances Cabrini did.

Francis of Assisi

This is the saint who got the idea to put a Christmas crib scene in church every year! And today most Catholic churches—AND homes—copy Francis' idea each Christmas. BUT when Francis was a young man, he only had ONE idea. He just wanted to have a good time!

Francis was the son of a rich man, and he LIKED leading the life of a rich man's son! But when he decided to CHANGE his life, he changed it dramatically! Instead of wearing expensive clothes, he wore a simple brown robe and sometimes even gave away his shoes and went barefoot. He became a monk, prayed a lot, and was a friend to everyone—even the animals.

And then one Christmas he got the idea that he should try to help people FEEL like they were THERE when Jesus was born in a stable. So he got busy, building and arranging, and when people came in church that night for Midnight Mass, they saw a Christmas crib scene—with Baby Jesus, Mary, and Joseph. BUT Francis' crib was a little different from those of today because he even brought some of his REAL animal friends into church to stand by the crib!

Francis, the rich man's son, learned to love God and ALL his creatures. AND, just like when he was young, he spent his life having a GOOD time—just a different KIND of good time!

Everybody likes to have a good time! But SOME people have the idea that means wild parties and doing things that are NOT good! What is YOUR idea of having a GOOD time?

Gall

Do you like to go fishing? Then you should make friends with this saint because he spent a lot of time fishing! He also spent a lot of time preaching and converting people to Christianity, but whenever he had any spare time, he spent it knotting fishing nets and sitting on the bank of a river or lake enjoying the sport of fishing.

Gall was born in Ireland. He was a friend of Saint Columban and traveled around with him preaching and teaching. In his later life, he became a hermit and spent his days in prayer—but it is noted that the place where he lived was very near a river that was known to be a good fishing spot!

It's easy to think that saints did nothing but pray, but many of them also liked to fish, sing songs, play ball, and all the ordinary things that YOU might like to do too. The big difference is that many people today spend ALL their time doing things like fishing, singing songs, playing ball, and watching TV and NEVER save even a little bit of time each day to pray. YOU would never do that, would you?

Genesius the Comedian

Did you ever watch a comedian on TV or in the movies? They are sooo funny that they make you giggle and guffaw, chuckle and chortle. Well, legend says that is what Genesius did as a career. He appeared with a group of players and put on funny plays.

One day Genesius and his group were asked to put on an "entertainment" for the emperor—a very important assignment. They got the bright idea to put on a play making fun of Christians! At that time Christians were considered foolish people, and they were also people in danger because the emperor had all Christians killed. So Genesius and his friends knew the Romans would laugh if they made fun of Christians!

When the play began, Genesius would pretend that HE wanted to become a Christian and be baptized. He would make it look very funny. And then some other actors would come in and pretend to be priests and go through fancy rituals baptizing him.

But an even funnier thing happened! In the middle of the play when Genesius said he wanted to be baptized, he was suddenly filled with a great love of God and truly DID want to become a Christian! When the play was over, he told everyone that God had touched him and he was sorry he had made fun of Christianity and he hoped everyone else would also believe in Jesus Christ.

Genesius had tried to play a joke on God. Instead, God played a happy joke on Genesius!

Did you ever play a joke on someone? Was it a funny joke or a MEAN joke? God gave you the wonderful gift of laughter, AND he filled the world with lots of things for you to laugh about—giraffes with long funny necks and turtles with short funny necks that fit inside a shell, puppy dogs and kitty cats that do such silly things, monkeys that make funny faces and people who make funny faces too! The next time you have a really good giggle, tell God thanks for comedians like Saint Genesius AND for the gift of laughter.

Genevieve

This saint was a shepherd-girl and a vegetarian and is said to have SAVED the city of Paris!

When Genevieve was just a little girl, she spent most of her days with other children tending the flocks of sheep who grazed on Mount Valerien in France. When she was only fifteen, she became a nun AND a vegetarian! As a sacrifice, she often fasted, eating only bread and beans, and NEVER ate meat.

One time the people of Paris heard that Attila the Hun and his armies of cruel barbarians were coming to capture the city. Many people wanted to run for their lives and abandon the city, but Genevieve told them to stay in their homes. She told them to pray and fast, asking God to save the city. Following her example, many of the

Um... Let's go this way instead.

people DID stay and pray. And after many days of prayer, Attila suddenly changed the direction of his march and did NOT come to Paris. The city was saved, and the people never forgot. Saint Genevieve is now the patron saint of Paris.

Attila the Hun is known as one of the most brutal warriors in history. No wonder the people of Paris were afraid of him! Do YOU know anyone who is mean like Attila—a school bully, a cruel neighbor, a relative with a terrible temper? You should probably try to keep out of that person's way, but it would ALSO be a good idea to PRAY for the brute!

George

Have you ever heard the story of Saint George slaying the dragon? It is a purely legendary story, like a fairy tale, and there may be NO truth to it, but it IS a wonderful story.

According to the legend, George was a Christian knight (in shining armor and probably riding a white horse)! He happened to be traveling through a city when he met a group of people, and they told him that their city was in terror of a horrible dragon who ATE one of their citizens each day!

The people said that they had put all their names down on a slip of paper and each day they would draw one name and that person would have to go out to be eaten—and that very day, the name drawn was that of their beloved princess. George immediately went out and fought the terrible dragon and killed him, saving the princess and the whole town.

This story is so popular that it has been used in books, cartoons, and even on postage stamps! In fact, the picture of Saint George has been used on more stamps and in more countries than that of any other saint!

Do you ever NOTICE the pictures on postage stamps? Some of them are very special. That's why so many people are stamp COLLECTORS. Do YOU have any kind of collection—shells, marbles, baseball cards? What about HOLY cards? There are many beautiful holy cards that have pictures of Jesus, Mary, and the saints. If you ever go to a religious store, ask to see some holy cards, and maybe you'll find one with a picture of Saint George and his dragon!

Gregory the Great (Pope)

You know about rock music and rap music and maybe even elevator music—but did you ever hear of Gregorian chant? Well, that was a beautiful chant once sung in church, and it was named after this saint—although he probably didn't have anything to do with music, since he was very busy with other matters.

In fact, he did so many OTHER things that he became known as Gregory the GREAT! At one time Gregory was the richest man in Rome. Then he decided to give all his money to the Church and became a monk. He wanted to live a quiet life, but he was known to be so talented that he kept getting named to prestigious positions and finally became pope.

Gregory had a fine sense of justice and treated all with charity and humility. He had to battle many enemies of the Church but was never too busy to care about individuals. One of the last things he did before he died was to send a warm cloak to a poor friend who was suffering from the cold. Gregory was the first pope to call himself "Servant of the servants of God."

 Do you know anyone who is so smart or good or wise or successful that you could call him or her "The Great"? Think about that today—and then think what YOU might like to do someday so that people could call YOU "The Great"!

Gregory the Wonder-Worker

This saint became bishop of a town where there were only SEVENTEEN Christians! His work—and wonders—changed that.

The very first day Gregory arrived in the town where he would be bishop, he went right out and started preaching. He was such a good preacher that quite a few of his listeners decided to become Christians! By the next morning, the town was abuzz with news about him, and more and more came to listen to him and soon there were LOTS of Christians in town. And they all got together and gave their time and/or money to help Gregory build a church where they could pray together.

During his years as bishop, legend says that Gregory—by the power of God—was able to heal the sick, change the course of rivers, drive out evil spirits, and foretell the future! And that's how he got his name, the Wonder-Worker.

After many years of work—and wonders—Gregory grew old and knew he was dying. He asked how many people in his town were still NOT Christians. He was told there were only SEVENTEEN!

When Gregory became bishop, only seventeen WERE Christians and now only seventeen were NOT! He had done his work well.

How many Christians live in YOUR town? Are there lots or just a few? How many are there in your neighborhood or your family? And how about wonder-workers? Are there any of THOSE in your town? It's fun to watch magicians work wonders, but THEIR magic is a TRICK. Only God's "magic" is real! Say a prayer today to thank God for the "magic" of thunderclaps and hands to clap, watermelons and waterfalls—and wonder-workers like Gregory.

Helena

This saint was just the daughter of an innkeeper, but then she became a SOMEBODY, then a nobody, then a SOMEBODY again!

When Helena was young and beautiful, she met an important Roman general; and even though she was from a "lowly" family, the general married her, and they had a son named Constantine.

A few years later the emperor named Helena's husband to be "Caesar," the top Roman ruler! Then, for political reasons, Helena's husband decided to divorce HER and marry the emperor's stepdaughter—and Helena became a nobody again. BUT the story was not over. Just thirteen years later, Helena's husband died and her son, Constantine, became the ruler! NOW Constantine demanded that everyone give great honor to his mother, and he even had some Roman coins made with her picture on them.

It was Constantine who issued the edict that allowed Christianity to be practiced as a religion in the Roman Empire, and he released all those who had been put in prison because of their religion. Helena began to study about Christianity and decided to BECOME a Christian. After that, she worked very hard for the Church. She traveled all over Palestine, built many churches, and became known for her kindness to prisoners, soldiers, and the poor.

Legend tells us that while she was traveling in the Holy Land, it was Saint Helena who found the true cross on which Jesus had been crucified.

Didn't this saint have an interesting life? Would YOU like to travel to the Holy Land and see the places where Jesus lived, the roads where he walked, the city where he was crucified? Well, maybe you can't do that right now but maybe you will SOME DAY. RIGHT NOW you COULD go to the library and get out a book about the Holy Land and see the pictures of those places and READ all about them. Why don't you do that?

Hilarion

This saint's name sounds hilarious, doesn't it? But he was actually a very serious man who RAN from FAME!

Saint Hilarion was a hermit who wanted to be left ALONE to live a quiet, prayerful life in his little hut in Palestine. BUT people began to hear that Hilarion's prayers brought about miracles, and soon so many people came to ask him to pray for them that Hilarion decided he would have to MOVE to escape the crowds!

Hilarion went to Egypt; but his fame followed him there, and soon his quiet hermitage was AGAIN besieged by people. Hilarion next went to Sicily and then to Dalmatia and then to Cyprus. Everywhere he went, holy Hilarion's prayers resulted in miracles—and MORE people!

Movie stars and rock stars usually have LOTS of people following them, but you seldom hear about a HERMIT being pursued by crowds! Hilarion must have been one special hermit! Do you happen to know anyone who would LIKE to be a hermit—and live all alone in a little hut in the desert or in a wilderness? Do any members in your family ever tell you to "Leave me alone" or "Please be QUIET "? Maybe they really MEAN it. Some people DO like peace and quiet!

Hildegard of Bingen

This saint could read, but she never learned to write Latin—which was required for writers in her day.

Hildegard was a nun, an abbess, a musician, and an artist. She had ideas about many subjects and wanted to "communicate" them to others. She became known as a writer because she dictated her thoughts to those who wrote them down for her.

Hildegard wrote on many subjects—natural history, medicine, plants, animals, reptiles, headaches, insanity, and even blood circulation. And her writings on religious subjects included commentaries on the Bible and the saints, hymns, poems, and even a morality play.

She also wrote LOTS of letters—and got lots BACK from popes, kings, archbishops, teachers, abbots, monks, and nuns.

It must have been very difficult for a woman with so many ideas in her head to NOT be able to write them down, to always have to wait until she could dictate them to someone else. In spite of that, this non-writer touched many with her writings!

Would YOU like to be a writer some day? It's a wonderful way to share your ideas with the world. So aren't you lucky that you already know how to write? Of course, even if you don't WANT to be a writer, you can still be a sharer. It can be fun to share ANYTHING with someone else—except maybe a candy bar! Think of someone today with whom you might like to share a secret—or an idea or a game or maybe even a candy bar. Then do it!

Homobonus

This saint was a good businessman—AND a good man. In fact, in Latin, *homo bonus* MEANS "good man"!

The father of Homobonus was a merchant, and he taught his son all about his business so that when Homobonus was old enough, he could be his father's partner. Homobonus learned his lessons well. His father taught him that to be a good businessman, he must be a good man—honest, fair, dutiful, just, and kind.

Homobonus lived his whole business life that way, treating customers as he would like to be treated himself. And he lived his

private life the same way. He married a lady who was prudent and faithful as he was, and they gave much of the money they made from their successful business to those who were less fortunate.

Homobonus went to Mass every day. After many years—when he was a very old man—he suddenly collapsed during Mass. He died as he had lived—at prayer. A "good man" to the end.

Would YOU like to be a GOOD businessperson some day? Maybe run a restaurant, shoe store, real estate office, or lawn-mowing service? SOME people today think the BEST way to be successful in business is to be dishonest and cheat the customers. Others know better. Think about business today and HOW MANY DIFFERENT KINDS of businesses SERVE your family—grocery stores, electric and gas companies, automobile service stations, clothing stores, movies, TV repair shops. This list goes on and on— and you want them ALL to TREAT YOU FAIRLY. So if you ever go into business, always treat OTHERS as YOU would like to be treated. Remember, HOMOBONUS! To be a good business person, FIRST be a good person!

Ignatius of Loyola

This saint was barely five feet tall—but at that height, he was still taller than Napoleon or Julius Caesar! And all three "little" men made a big mark in history!

Ignatius was born in a castle in Spain in 1491, one year before the queen and king of Spain sent Columbus sailing off to discover America! Since Ignatius was a member of a noble family, he became a courtier (an attendant at a royal court) and a soldier. When he was fighting to defend the castle at Pamplona, his leg was shattered by a cannonball—and his life changed.

While recuperating from the wound, Ignatius read a lot of religious books and decided to become a missionary. He left his sword at a shrine of the Blessed Mother and exchanged his fine clothes for those of a beggar. He lived in a CAVE for a year,

praying and writing. He went back to school for a while and then left Spain to go to Paris, where he and a few friends formed a group known as the Society of Jesus.

Ignatius did not plan to found a new religious order but a group of "commandos" who could respond quickly and go out on "missions" to preach and work wherever or whenever they were needed. The pope approved this new idea, and Ignatius' band of "apostolic adventurers" grew from ten to one thousand in a few short years and eventually spread to many countries. The Society of Jesus (also known as the Jesuits) became one of the Church's greatest religious organizations—all because of a cannonball!

You've probably thought about being an adventurer some time, but did you ever think about being an "apostolic adventurer"? Did you ever think about some day going whenever and wherever you are needed to help, to preach, and to educate others about God and the Catholic Church? Many young people today still do the kind of work Ignatius and his friends did—they become priests, Sisters, and, yes, missionaries and apostolic adventurers! Would YOU like to do that some day?

Isidore of Seville

Did you ever use an encyclopedia to "look up" some fact or some historical person? Well, who do you think puts together an encyclopedia? One person who did is Saint Isidore!

Isidore was known as the most learned man of his time, AND in addition to building schools, writing MANY scholarly books, living a SAINTLY life, and serving as BISHOP of Scville, he put together an encyclopedia.

Isidore's encyclopedia included all the knowledge of his day and was used for hundreds of years as a school textbook. BUT Isidore's DAY was the sixth century—over fourteen hundred years ago—so his encyclopedia was very different from the ones found in today's schools. Isidore's book could not have included information about telephones, television, airplanes, space travel, electric lights, microwave ovens, or many of the everyday things YOU take for grantcd. Wouldn't this saint have been surprised if he could have seen a twentieth-century encyclopedia?

How often do you USE an encyclopedia to get information or maybe "fun facts"? You should try it morc often! In fact, why don't you sit down with an encyclopedia today and look up some subjects that might be especially interesting to you. As you thumb through the pages, you might even come upon the name of Isidore of Seville!

Isidore the Farmer

This Isidore was actually named after the learned Isidore who wrotc the encyclopedia— but they lived VERY different lives.

This Isidore was born to a poor family in Spain, and as soon as he was old enough to go to work, he became a farm laborer, working for a wealthy man who had an estate outside the city. This was not just Isidore's first job—it was his ONLY job. He worked there on the farm all his life, getting up very early each morning to go to Mass and then spending his days in the fields.

Isidore married a girl as poor as he was, and together they lived a saintly Christian life. It is said that Isidore prayed all day as he plowed, and he was so generous to others that, as poor as he was, he gave generously to the even poorer. If he had nothing else to give, he would share his meal.

The two Isidores were very different in their lifestyles—but alike in their saintliness.

 Would YOU like to be a farmer? What would you grow—spinach and squash, rutabagas and radishes, carrots and cabbages, and YUMMY stuff like that? Too bad they don't have chocolate-pie plants or cookie crops! You may choose a lifestyle very different from Isidore the Farmer OR Isidore the Encyclopedia Man—but you can remember them as a good example of how you can choose ANY kind of lifestyle and still be "saintly"!

James the Greater

Here's an apostle AND a saint who was the brother of an apostle and a saint AND was the first apostle to be martyred. So is that why he is called "the greater"? Nope.

There were TWO apostles named

James and this one was the older—so instead of being called James the Older, he was called James the Greater. But he was ALSO GREAT!

In fact, Jesus must have really like James because he gave him a funny nickname! Jesus called James and his brother John "Sons of Thunder"! Do you guess that was because they had LOUD personalities or NOISY voices or STORMY tempers?

Do you know anyone who might be called a son or daughter of thunder? A stormy temper can get you in A LOT of trouble! But maybe the apostles HAD to thunder to get people to listen to their important message about Jesus and his new religion. If YOU ever have trouble with your temper, you might ask Saint James to help you remember to speak softly, act kindly, and save your thunder for when you have something REALLY important to say—like Help! Fire! or Look Out!

James the Less

How would you like to have a name like "the less"? Well, as you have probably guessed by reading about James the Greater, in this case, *less* means "the younger"—and being young is a lot better than being less!

This younger James was a pretty important follower of Jesus. He was the Bishop of Jerusalem and is believed to be the author of the Epistle of James in the New Testament. Pretty good for someone known as "the less"!

Do you ever feel "less"—less smart than a friend, less strong than a schoolmate, less rich than a neighbor, or less energetic than the rest of your family? Does feeling less leave you listless? Well, don't let less get you down! Most people feel "less" at some times or on some days. So when you have one of those times or one of those days, remember that God thinks you are the "most"! Why? Because YOU are one of his creations, one of his children, one of his special friends. So hold your head high, lift up your spirit, and say, "I will be MORE than less. I will be grateful for all God has given me, and I will use those gifts to become MORE. No matter what happens or what anyone says to me, I will remember that God loves me and thinks I am the MOST!"

Jeanne Jugan

Would you like to have a job as a maid, working in the kitchen of a wealthy family? Well, that's the job Jeanne took when she was only sixteen years old.

Jeanne was one of eight children in a poor family that lived in a little fishing village in France. When she was only three years old, her fisherman father died in a storm at sea and her mother struggled to raise the family.

Jeanne went to work for a wealthy noblewoman, who was very generous and often took Jeanne with her when she went to deliver food and medicine to the poor and sick of the village. After a few years, when Jeanne was twenty-five, she went to work in a hospital where she cared for the sick, and then spent all her spare time helping the homeless and hungry who lived in the streets. Later, she again worked as a maid in the home of a wealthy woman and, this noblewoman also helped Jeanne feed the starving street people.

Eventually, Jeanne moved in with a seventy-year-old woman and a seventeen-year-old girl, and the three of them took in poor elderly women from the streets and gave them their own beds and begged for food to feed them. Soon other women began to help in this work, and volunteers raised money so they could move into an abandoned convent and repair it and use it as a place to care for the most helpless of the poor.

In 1842 this group of women formed a new religious community known as the Little Sisters of the Poor and elected Jeanne as their superior. She then took the name of Sister Mary of the Cross. More and more women joined the Order, and by the time Jeanne died, at the age of eighty-seven, there were hundreds of Little Sisters of the Poor working in many cities of the world.

In her later years, Sister Mary was no longer superior but was in charge of the very youngest sisters, who did the manual work in the convent, and many of the Sisters never even knew that this elderly Sister was the foundress of their Order.

Jeanne has not been named a saint yet, but she was "beatified" in 1982 and can now be called Blessed Sister Mary of the Cross.

Isn't it wonderful that a poor sixteen-year-old girl who began work as a maid could start by helping a few homeless people and then gather a group that has grown to help thousands of people all over the world? Don't ever think YOU are too poor or too young or too dumb to do something important! You can't just DREAM it or WISH it or THINK about it—but if you really want to do something and are willing to work and pray for it, you, too, CAN do something important!

Jerome

Evagrius

Heliodorus

Eusebius

BoNosus.

What's in a name? Well, Saint Jerome was really named Eusebius Hieronymus Sophronius. AND he had friends named Bonosus, Evagrius, Heliodorus, Epiphanius, and Eustochium! In spite of that, Jerome became one of the greatest, wisest saints.

Jerome was a secretary to a pope, became famous for his writing and translation of the Scriptures, and impressed the people of his time with his honesty, learning, and personal holiness. So the only name we need remember him by is "saint."

Although the names of his day may sound strange to you, maybe names you know today—Elvis, Robin, Whitney, Goldie, Kiefer, or Nicole—would sound just as strange to the people who lived back in the fourth and fifth centuries when Jerome did!

Do you ever wish you had a different name? If you could have chosen any name when you were born, what would that name have been? How about Glamouroso, Astronautus, Star, Richenfamous? Or how about Christian? Could people tell by the way you act that you ARE a Christian even though you weren't named that name? Should people be able to tell that? What could you do today to let someone know you ARE a Christian?

Joan of Arc

Did you know some people called this saint a WITCH? And do you know why?

Well, Joan was always a very prayerful, pious young girl, but when she was a teenager, she began to hear "voices." The voices told her that God wanted her to go to the commander of the French army and tell him that the French forces were going to suffer a serious defeat. The commander laughed at her and said her father should give her a good spanking!

Joan went back home, but she kept hearing the voices telling her that God wanted HER to LEAD the army. She said she was just a poor girl and couldn't even ride a horse, much less fight with an army. But the voices persisted. Finally, she went back to see the commander again. This time he listened to her BECAUSE the French HAD been defeated just as Joan had predicted. Joan was sent to see Charles, whose father had been king of France but whose coronation had been postponed because of the war. Charles tried to trick Joan by wearing a disguise, but she was able to recognize him immediately and gave him a secret signal, which convinced him of her sincerity. His advisers, however, thought she was either crazy or some kind of spy. They subjected Joan to THREE WEEKS of questioning before they decided she could be trusted.

Joan was outfitted with a suit of white armor, and a special flag was made with the words "Jesus and Mary" on it. Then she rode off to lead an army into battle and free the city of Orleans from the British. Joan was successful in several battles and regained enough French territory so that Charles could be crowned king—with Joan standing at his side.

In a later battle though, Joan was captured by the enemy, put in prison, accused of being a "witch," and burned at the stake! Because of her bravery and holiness, this young girl became known as the Maid of Orleans and SAINT Joan of Arc.

Probably the only "witches" you will ever meet are the ones you see at Halloween! But you COULD meet some "saints." In fact, you may have already met some! Think about it. Do you know any saints? Do you know any people who are brave and holy? Do you know any people who pray a lot and love God a lot and are not AFRAID to say that God is their friend? Well, maybe you DO know some saints. And maybe you could try to be more saintly yourself!

John Bosco

Would you expect a saint to be an acrobat, a juggler, a magician? Well, John Bosco was all of those!

His main work was to help poor boys—to teach them a trade so they could earn a living and to teach them about God so they could have a happy life. He himself knew what it was like to be poor. When John Bosco entered the seminary to become a priest, he had to rely on charity for his priestly clothes. He got a cloak from the parish priest, a cassock from a parishioner, a pair of shoes from a friend, and his hat from the mayor!

When John Bosco first started working with the boys, they were a rowdy lot. John tried to be strict, but they paid little attention—so then he decided to be fun. Each Sunday he would have a combination lesson-play time. He would mix his funny acrobatic stunts and magic tricks in with the lessons, and the boys would laugh and learn at the same time.

Finally, John Bosco was able to get enough money to open a HOME for boys PLUS a workshop to teach them to become shoemakers and tailors. His mother, "Mama Margaret," helped and soon others helped too. Within a few years, his followers had spread all across the world, opening homes to help poor boys get a good start in life. But probably none of John's followers were as good acrobats, jugglers, and magicians as their saintly leader!

> Do YOU think that to be a good Catholic, you have to be somber and serious, always praying but never laughing? Well, think again! A Christian should be FILLED with the joy of God—so follow the example of John Bosco and put on a happy face!

John Eudes

Can you imagine a saint living in a large wine cask out in the middle of a field? Well, that's what THIS saint did for a while.

John was a priest working in Normandy when a terrible plague broke out there.

He volunteered to help care for the sick and dying, even though he knew the plague was very contagious and he COULD catch it and die himself. This didn't bother him, BUT he didn't want to take the chance of infecting the other priests in his religious community, soooo, when he was not on nursing duty, John slept and lived in the large wine cask!

After the plague passed, John returned to his community and became known for many good works—preaching parish missions, running seminaries, writing books. He wrote his last book when he was seventy-nine years old and finished it just one month before he died.

Have you ever seen a wine cask big enough to hold a man? Some of the really BIG ones in France look like huge barrels and would be big enough to live in—IF you could be satisfied with VERY close quarters! John was content to settle for that because he cared about OTHERS more than about himself. Do you know anyone that unselfish? Someone who puts OTHERS first instead of always thinking ME FIRST and YOU LAST? Maybe YOU'RE like Saint John Eudes—or maybe you COULD be.

John Gualbert

This saint planned to MURDER someone for revenge! But he changed his mind.

When his BROTHER was murdered, John set out to get even. Filled with hatred and revenge, he tracked down his brother's killer and drew out a sword to kill him. But just as he was about to strike the fatal blow, the man begged for mercy.

John suddenly realized what he was doing. He had hated this man for being a murderer, and now HE was going to be a murderer himself! He forgave the man he had despised. THEN John put away his sword and went to a monastery to became a monk!

He prayed and worked and became known for his many good deeds and his spiritual wisdom—and great crowds came seeking his advice. The almost-murderer became a for-sure saint!

Did you ever get so mad at somebody, you wanted REVENGE? You wanted to get even? If that ever happens, remember this saint and calm down, chill out, think it over. Do YOU want to be as bad as the person who made you mad? In the Our Father, we ask God to forgive us "as we forgive others." So if YOU want to be forgiven, then YOU have to be ready to forgive others. Think about that today and then say an Our Father.

John Neumann

Did you know that this saint is sometimes called the "Father of the American Catholic Education System"? Yep, John Neumann BELIEVED in Catholic schools.

He was born in Bohemia and wanted to become a priest. But he was denied ordination because there were TOO MANY priests in Bohemia. So John journeyed to New York to be ordained and later joined the Redemptorist Congregation. America was a strange new land for him. He had come from a country SO Catholic they had TOO MANY priests to a land that in some ways was anti-Catholic.

As he traveled around doing missionary work, John met many immigrants who were from Catholic countries like he was. BUT they had found that in America, there were not so many Catholic churches or schools where they could worship and learn. John set out to change that. He wanted to be sure all Catholic children could get a good education AND learn about their faith as he had.

When John became a bishop, he tried to open a Catholic school in EVERY parish of his diocese. Because of his work—and that of others who shared his educational goals—the Catholic school system spread all over the United States.

> Do you LIKE to go to school? Or not? How do you think a PERFECT school would be? Would it start at dawn and END at noon? Or START at noon and end at dark? Would there be a dress code, homework, field trips? What would the teachers be like? Think today of how YOU would plan a school—NOT just one that would be fun but ALSO one that would give you basic teachings AND values AND inspiration to help you become a wise and GOOD adult.

John of Capistrano

This saint was born in the famous town of Capistrano, but he may have never become famous himself—as a saint—if he had not gone to prison!

During a war, John was captured and thrown into prison. While he sat there with nothing to do, John began to think about how he had spent his life. He decided he had not just SPENT it, he had WASTED it. When John got out of prison, legend says that he rode through town seated backward on a DONKEY, facing the TAIL of the donkey!

AND he was wearing a huge paper hat on which he had written all of his worst sins! People stared and children threw things at him, but this was John's way of showing he was sorry for his sins.

He rode that donkey right to a monastery, where he asked to enter and become a monk. After he studied and prayed, John began to preach and tell people how he had changed his life to get closer to God. Thousands of people came to hear him, and many of them decided to change THEIR lives too.

Are you surprised to hear that a saint would ride a donkey and wear a paper hat? Well, YOU don't have to ride a donkey to tell God you're sorry for the bad things you've done. You can just sit very quietly (like John did in prison) and think about what bad habits you have or how you would like to act better. Then say a little prayer and talk to God about it. Why don't you do that right now!

John of the Many!

WOULD YOU BELIEVE there are SEVENTY saints officially recorded with the name of John? And there are probably many more "saintly" Johns who are NOT recorded!

The first Saint John was, of course, John the Apostle, said to be a good friend and the "favorite" apostle of Jesus. A recent "saintly" John is, of course, Pope John Paul II.

And in between there have been John the Good, John the Silent, John the Almsgiver, John the Spaniard, John of Nicodemia, John of Perugia, John of the Marches, John of the Grating—and LOTS more.

What a saintly name this is!

Do YOU have a saintly name? Or an unusual name? Or a popular name? Or a name you hate? Well, you'll never have to take the blame for your name—since somebody else gave it to you! If you like it, flaunt it. If you don't like it, change it! But you DO have to take the blame for the way you use GOD's name. Some people throw it around, using it casually, sarcastically, and NOT reverently. You would never do that, would you?

Joseph

The Bible tells us that Joseph was a good and just man— and that's about it. But that's enough to make this quiet man the favorite saint of many.

We DO know that Joseph took care of Mary and Jesus. When there was "no room in the inn," Joseph found shelter for Mary in a stable. When Jesus was born, Joseph was there.

When an angel told Joseph the Baby Jesus was in danger, Joseph bravely left his home and took Jesus and Mary to the safety of Egypt. When it was time to present the Baby Jesus to be blessed at the Temple, Joseph was there.

When Jesus was twelve years old and got "lost," Joseph went with Mary, searching until they found him. As Jesus grew up, whenever he needed a fatherly, helping hand, Joseph was there.

Not much is known about the life of this saint except that when he was needed, Joseph was there.

There are many "good and just" people in the world, but their stories are seldom seen on the front page of the newspaper or on the TV news. You see and hear all about rock stars and movie stars, but how often do you hear about the people who quietly go about their lives, working, helping, "being there" when they are needed? Say a prayer of thanksgiving today and EVERY day for all the GOOD parents, grandparents, teachers, plumbers, priests, electricians, garbage collectors, police officers, doctors, farmers, school-bus drivers—all the "saints" of TODAY!

Joseph of Cupertino

Did you know there is a patron saint of astronauts? Yep! This is the saint. There are several saints named Joseph, but this one was a person who started out as a real "loser"!

His family was so poor that their house had to be sold to pay their debts, and Joseph was born in a shack. As a child, he was so absent-minded that everyone made fun of him. He went to work as a shoemaker's helper but was so bad at the job, he got fired. Then he tried to join a monastery, but the superiors refused to take him so he joined another one. He was so bad at his job there that they asked him to leave after only eight months. Finally, he was accepted at a third monastery and was put to work in the stables. Here he worked so hard and was so prayerful and kind that he was finally accepted to study for the priesthood.

After Joseph became a priest, he continued to do simple, routine duties but spent most of his time in prayer. Many people reported miracles of healing when Joseph prayed for them. Over seventy times, people SAW Joseph praying so hard that, while he was praying, he actually ROSE from the floor and was suspended in the air! This is known as "levitation" and it is one reason Joseph was named the patron of astronauts!

Would you like to be an astronaut? Or would you like to be a saint? Well, maybe you could even be BOTH! And if you ever feel like a "loser," just think about Joseph of Cupertino —a man who seemed destined to fail but instead "rose" to great heights as a saint.

Jude (Thaddeus)

I'm Jude! Not Judas!

Did you ever get blamed for something you didn't do? That's a terrible feeling, isn't it? Well, Jude had a name that SOUNDED like Judas—the apostle who betrayed Jesus—so it would be easy to get him confused and blame him for something he did NOT do. Jude was NOT a traitor; in fact, he was a very good disciple who worked to spread the teachings of Christianity. He is mentioned in the Bible, but in some places, he is called Thaddeus, so it is easy to get him confused with another saint who was also named Thaddeus!

All this confusion may be the reason Jude is known as the patron of people who are in HOPELESS situations. MAYBE—since Jude sounded so much like Judas and NOBODY would want to ask Judas for help, people would ask everybody else first, and THEN, when all else failed and the situation was HOPELESS, they would ask Jude and he would help them!

Have you ever been in a HOPELESS situation? Maybe you wanted to learn to swim, but no matter how hard you tried, you just couldn't keep from sinking! Maybe you wanted to be friends with someone, but he or she did NOT want to be friends with you. Or maybe you wanted to DO something special, but you just couldn't decide WHAT that would be! Well, the next time you get in a HOPELESS situation, pray to Saint Jude, begging him to ask God to help you find an answer or a way out. It may take a while, since this is such a confusing saint—but when all seems hopeless anyway, it couldn't hurt to ask for help!

Kateri Tekakwitha

Did you know there was an American Indian who is known as the "Lily of the Mohawks"—an Indian maiden who was baptized as a Christian on Easter Sunday and made her first Communion on Christmas day?

Kateri was orphaned as a child and grew up with the Mohawks, living the typical Indian life. But when she was twenty years old, she met a missionary priest who told her about Christianity, and Kateri asked to be baptized. After that, the other Indians were furious at what she had done and were mean to her and treated her like an outcast.

Afraid for her life, Kateri decided to leave the Mohawks and try to find a Christian Indian village she had heard about. She started out, all alone, and walked TWO HUNDRED MILES through the Canadian wilderness—but she found the village! She was safe there and was a good and holy Christian for the rest of her life. In 1980 she was named "Blessed Kateri" by Pope John Paul II.

> Would YOU be afraid to travel two hundred miles all alone through the wilderness? Most people would be—and Kateri was probably afraid too; but, with God's help, she did what she had to do. The next time you have to do something you're afraid to do, think of Kateri, ask God to help you— and then do what you have to do!

Lawrence the Deacon

This saint played a joke on a Roman ruler! But the Roman was NOT amused.

Lawrence was ordained by Pope Sixtus to be one of seven deacons in Rome in the third century. One of his jobs was to be sort of an accountant—to keep track of the "treasures" people donated to the Church AND to use the money to pay for the upkeep of the church buildings and ministers AND to help the poor. This was a big job, since the Church of Rome took care of more than fifteen hundred poor people in the city and also sent money to help the poor in other cities.

One day the Emperor Valerian began a great persecution of the Church and issued orders for all the priests and bishops to be killed, including the pope!

As the pope was being led away to be executed, he told Lawrence to give ALL the riches of the Church to the poor. So Lawrence began to sell everything and give away the money. BUT the prefect (chief magistrate) of Rome heard about this and was furious because he had expected to TAKE the treasures for the empire.

Treasures?

He sent for Lawrence and ordered him to bring all the Church's treasures to HIM. Lawrence agreed but said it would take three days to assemble the treasures. Three days later, Lawrence appeared before the prefect. Instead of bringing gold and silver, he had brought the crippled, the blind, the poor, and the orphans of the city. Lawrence said THESE were the real "treasures" of the Church.

The prefect was even more furious and had his soldiers torture and kill Lawrence. But Lawrence had expected the ruler to react this way and gladly gave his life for God. AND when people heard what Lawrence had done, this gave them courage to ALSO stand up to the Romans. Many new converts asked to be baptized, and the Church grew and Catholicism spread across the country.

Did you ever think of the poor as a "treasure"? Would you like to work to help the poor some day? Well, why not TODAY? Could you get your family to have a garage sale and give all the money to help the poor? Could you get your friends to gather together any unused clothing or toys and donate them to an organization that helps the poor? Could you get your grandma to make cookies so you could sell them door to door and give your "profit" to the poor? What COULD you do to get some "treasure" to help the poor in YOUR city or your neighborhood?

Leo IX (Pope)

Could you imagine a pope commanding an army? That's what Leo did! He led an army against Norman invaders, and THEN he was captured and put in prison.

Before that war, Leo had already earned a reputation as a busy and holy pope, traveling all over Western Europe, making necessary reforms in the Church, being a peacemaker between the emperor and the king, and ruling wisely and well.

That's why SOME fussed at Leo, saying he had other work to do, and a pope should not be a military commander leading an army! But at that time, there were many WARS against Christianity, and Leo must have felt he should defend the Church in ALL ways, against ALL enemies.

In fact, an earlier Leo—Pope Leo IV who had been the pope two hundred years before THIS Leo—had built a WALL around Saint Peter's Cathedral and Vatican Hill, trying to protect the Church from military invasions.

Throughout history, the Catholic Church has always had enemies. In earlier times, they attacked the Church with armies. Today, they often use words.

Are you surprised to find out how many different KINDS of popes there have been? Do you know how MANY popes there have been since the first pope, Saint Peter? There have been LOTS—including Linus, Sixtus, Hyginus, Telesphorus, Urban, Zosimus, Simplicius, Agapitus, and many who DID NOT have such strange names! Why don't you get a *Catholic Almanac* and look up ALL the popes and find out how many had funny names and how many didn't!

96

Louis Bertrand

When this saint was a teenager, he organized a "gang" of young people. But you'll never guess where they hung out!

Louis was born in Valencia, Spain. When he was growing up with his eight brothers and sisters, he was influenced by the deep religious faith and love of his parents. Even as a youngster, he wanted to follow their example.

His family prayed together every day, and Louis also began to pray alone in his room. Then, when he was a teenager, where do you think he took the "gang" he organized? Louis took them to local hospitals—to visit the sick!

Louis knew he wanted to become a priest, BUT he made bad grades in school, so he was afraid he'd be rejected. When he was eighteen, he applied anyway and was ACCEPTED by the Dominicans.

After he was ordained, the Dominican superior was so impressed with Louis that he made him the "novice master"—in charge of training young seminarians. Although he took "time out" a few years later to spend seven years as a missionary in South America, Louis returned to Spain and was novice master of their "gang" of young Dominicans for thirty years.

Have you ever known anyone who belonged to a "gang"? There are many young people today who belong to BAD gangs—who use drugs, destroy property, fight, and even kill people. Why don't YOU organize a GOOD DAY gang like Louis did? You wouldn't have to visit hospitals, but you COULD visit people in your neighborhood. Instead of doing something destructive, you could do something CONstructive. You could ask around and find out who really NEEDS a helping hand. Then you and your friends could offer to cut grass, shovel snow, clean out a garage, work in a garden, sweep a porch, do errands, or just visit with somebody who's lonely. Maybe they'll even give you a cookie to say thanks! But whether they do or not, you'll KNOW that you've made a difference—and that's the WAY for you and your gang to have a GOOD DAY!

Ludmila

You might say this lady became a saint because she was a good grandma! (Or maybe because she could spell all the names of the people in her family!) Ludmila was married to a duke named Borivoy. They had two sons named Spytihinev and Ratislav. And Ratislav and his wife, Drahomira, had a son named Wenceslaus. (Could YOU spell all those names?)

Well, anyway, when Borivoy decided to become a Christian, Ludmila asked to be baptized also and together they built the first Christian church in Bohemia.

But then Borivoy died and Ratislav became the duke. His wife was not a very good Christian, so Ludmila decided to take charge of her grandson and teach him all about God and Christianity. The people loved Ludmila because she was so kind and good to them, and Wenceslaus learned a lot from his grandma's good example. All was well until Ratislav died too! Then the leaders of an anti-Christian party saw their chance to try to take over the government, and they were afraid of the influence Ludmila had over her grandson. So one night, two men sneaked into the castle and killed her! But Ludmila had taught her grandson how to be a good Christian, so Wenceslaus supported God's law and his Church and ruled with justice and mercy.

Did you ever hear the song about Good King Wenceslaus? Sing that song today, and remember the ruler who learned a lot from his saintly grandma!

Luke

Would you like to see a picture of Mary, Jesus' mother? Well, legend says that Saint Luke painted a portrait of Mary, and if that was true, you could look at it and see exactly how our Blessed Mother looked. Unfortunately, no one knows if that is true or not, so you will just have to use your imagination to "picture" Mary in your heart and head.

We DO know that Luke was a friend of Saint Paul's, a doctor and a Greek who had a home in Antioch. Luke tells of his journeys with Saint Paul in the Acts of the Apostles in the Bible. Since Saint Paul was often in ill health, Luke probably was his personal doctor, who prescribed treatment for him and made the great Saint Paul "take his medicine."

Do you just hate to take medicine? Do you wrinkle your nose and hide under the covers and SEAL your mouth shut? Or do you make a terrible face and then hold your nose and open your mouth and swallow the stuff because you know it might make you feel better? Well, maybe you might like to be a doctor some day—like Saint Luke—and then you could make OTHER people take their medicine.

Lydia

This saint liked the "color purple."

Lydia lived in Thyatira, in the west central portion of the Roman province of Asia—a district that was famous for its purple dyes. At that time, purple was considered a "royal" color, and any material dyed that color was rare and expensive.

Lydia had a flourishing business,

selling items of the "color purple." Then one day, she heard Saint Paul preaching. Lydia was so impressed that she became Paul's FIRST Christian convert in that area. And then she had her whole household listen to Paul, and they ALL became Christians!

Lydia became famous as the "purple lady" whose story of conversion is told in the biblical book called the Acts of the Apostles.

> Do you have anything that is purple? Did you see the movie titled *The Color Purple?* Did you ever try to DYE anything purple? A lot of people dye Easter eggs purple, and a lot of people WEAR purple clothes. Whenever you see purple, think of Lydia and how she listened to Paul and was willing to change her whole life. In fact, why don't you honor Lydia by making TODAY a purple day? Put on purple socks, eat a purple grape, or make up a prayer and write it down with a purple crayon!

Margaret of Scotland

This saint found a husband by being shipwrecked! Margaret and her family had to flee Hungary when it was invaded by William the Conqueror. They were shipwrecked on the rocky coast of Scotland and were befriended by King Malcolm, III, who welcomed them to his country—and was so taken by Margaret's beauty and graciousness, he asked her to marry him!

Margaret accepted, and they were married in the castle of Dunfermline. Although he was a good man, Malcolm was rough and uncultured, like his country was at that time—but Margaret's influence softened his temper, polished his manners, and helped him become a just ruler.

Malcolm often consulted Margaret about the affairs of state, and she tried to improve her "adopted" country by promoting art and education AND religious reforms. Together, the royal couple built several churches.

Margaret and Malcolm had six sons and two daughters, so she

was a very busy mother and queen, but she always saved time in her private life to pray, read the Bible, and attend Mass. And she never sat down to eat without FIRST giving food to the orphans and beggars who came to her castle for help.

Fleeing from an invader and being shipwrecked took Margaret on a journey to a happy family and a saintly life.

Can you imagine how scary it would be to have to LEAVE your country and then to be shipwrecked and have to make a new home in a strange and foreign land? You don't have to be shipwrecked to know about change. Today, you see LOTS of change—moving from town to town, neighborhood to neighborhood, school to school, job to job. ANY change can be frightening—but also exciting. Have YOU ever had to make a big change in your life? Think today about what kind of change you would LIKE to make in your life. What could you DO to make that change happen?

Margaret Ward

This saint helped a "criminal" escape by smuggling a rope into prison in a basket of laundry!

Margaret lived in England at a time when Catholics were not permitted to practice their religion, and priests were not allowed—

under pain of death—to say Mass or even to enter the country. Margaret had helped hide and protect many priests, and when she went to the prison to visit the "criminal," Father William Watson, she brought him some clean clothes AND a rope!

The plan was set, and on a chilly damp night, Father Watson climbed from the prison window, carrying the rope. He inched his way across the prison roof, tied the rope securely, and let himself down. Margaret and a man who worked for her, John Roche, were waiting in the dark. They helped the priest get to the nearby river and make his escape by boat.

When the prison guards learned of the escape, the police soon suspected Margaret and John. They tracked them down and demanded that they tell where the priest was hiding. When both refused—even after being tortured—they were charged with high treason and hanged!

When you are watching those thrilling make-believe "adventures" on TV, think of the exciting REAL-LIFE adventures of some of the saints. They gave their hearts to God—and when it was necessary, they gave their lives.

Margaret Bourgeoys

Would you like to go to school in a stable? Well, that's where Saint Margaret taught!

She was born in France in a very "cultural" area, but she left there to travel as a missionary to a rugged wilderness area in Canada. Life

there was very difficult, but Margaret taught the women how to cook and sew and care for a family living in such a wild and untamed land. Then she asked the governor if she could have his stable. She cleaned it out and turned it into a schoolhouse! Margaret taught Indian children and children of the French settlers how to read, write, and count. AND she also taught them about God and told them how much God loved them.

Most of today's schools are very nice, clean, modern buildings; but throughout history, children have had to go to school in some very strange places—like Margaret's stable. Would YOU like to be a schoolteacher some day? Would you like to travel to a foreign land—maybe to a rugged wilderness—to be a missionary? Or how WOULD you like to spend the rest of your life? Think about that today, and start to plan and study so that some day you will have the "equipment"—the knowledge and education—to do whatever kind of work you want to do!

Maria Goretti

Would you believe the man who MURDERED Maria came to the ceremony when she was canonized a saint? It's true!

Maria was born on a small farm in Italy. Her mother said she was a happy, generous, open-hearted little girl who was never disobedient. When Maria was only nine years old, her father died, and after that, she helped take care of her six brothers and sisters and did some of the housework while her mother ran the farm.

When Maria was eleven years old—almost twelve—a neighbor boy named Alexander started noticing her and began to make sinful advances toward her. She fought him off but told no one because he said he would kill her AND her mother if she told. Finally, one day Alexander would not stop and started to attack Maria. She fought and screamed, crying out, "No, no, it's a sin. God does not want it."

Alexander went crazy with anger and fear and slashed out blindly at her with a knife, stabbing her several times. By the time help came and Maria was taken to the hospital, it was too late to save her. Before she died, she said she forgave Alexander and would pray for him.

Alexander was sent to prison, and it was eight years before Maria's prayers were answered. Then Alexander had a change of heart and reformed his life. He was finally released from prison for good behavior, twenty-seven years after the murder. The first place he went was to Maria's mother to beg her forgiveness. He then became a lay brother and lived a good and honorable life. Years later, Alexander was able to go to Rome—along with Maria's mother and brother and sisters—when the little girl he had murdered was canonized a saint.

Many of today's TV shows feature stories about people who lead immoral lives—and no one shouts, "No, no, it's a sin. God does not want it." If you ever see one of those TV shows, turn OFF that program and turn to a better one. THEN write a letter to the sponsors of the bad show and tell them, "No, no—you should NOT sponsor that kind of show. God does not want it."

Martin de Porres

This saint tried to help all God's lonely ones—orphans and slaves, the poor and the sick, and even stray cats and dogs!

Martin was born in Lima, Peru. His father was a Spanish knight, and his mother was a black freed-woman from Panama. When Martin was only twelve years old, he became an apprentice to a barber-surgeon. (At that time, barbers did not just give a shave and a haircut! They also treated the sick and dispensed medicines.)

After three years, Martin left that work to join the Dominicans— not to become a priest but to become a Brother. He continued to dispense medicine to the sick and was put in charge of giving out the convent's daily ration of food to the poor. He soon opened an orphanage and a hospital for foundlings (infants "found" after they were deserted by their parents). He also worked a great deal with the African slaves who had been brought in ships to Peru—visiting them on the docks to comfort them and to give them food and medicine.

It was said that Martin helped anyone who needed blankets, shirts, candles, miracles, or prayers! He even helped animals by providing a home for stray cats and dogs at his sister's house!

Martin is the patron saint of interracial justice.

Do you know anyone like Martin—someone ready to reach out a helping hand to whoever needs help whenever? Maybe YOU could be somebody like that. Think about it.

Mary, the Mother of Jesus

This special "saint" was surely the FIRST Christian. Mary was the FIRST to welcome Jesus into the world when she said YES to being his mother.

Mary was the one who cared for Jesus as a baby, saw him take his first steps, heard him say his first word. She cooked his meals, washed his clothes, and probably "kissed it to make it well" when he fell and got a scraped knee or stubbed his toe or got a boo-boo of a bruise.

Mary must have laughed with Jesus, and we know she cried for him when he was unjustly mocked, arrested, and crucified.

Mary rejoiced when her Son rose from the dead, and then she stayed with his friends, the apostles, and probably took care of THEM TOO when they started to preach the gospel of Christianity and began a new Church. Mary probably comforted them when people made fun of them just as they had ridiculed her Son.

But Mary was much MORE than a comforter. She was a LEADER. She was the FIRST to say YES. She was a strong but gentle influence in the early Church, as she is in today's Church. Mary is a role model for all ages.

Whenever YOU need a role model, someone to inspire you to be strong yet gentle, humble yet brave, look to Mary. Say "Hail Mary, full of grace—help ME to have the grace to be a good Catholic. The Lord is with thee AND with me; help ME to remember that. When God asked you to give your life to Jesus, you said YES—help ME to say yes too."

Matilda

This saint had a husband who was known as Henry, "the Fowler" because he liked to hunt hawks. She had three sons—one was an emperor, one was a duke, and one was an archbishop!

Matilda, who was sometimes called Maud, was the daughter of a duke and married a duke, who later became king of Germany. When she was the queen, both Matilda and her husband were very kind rulers—helping the poor and prisoners, teaching about God, and contributing money to many charitable causes.

After Henry died, two of Matilda's sons criticized her severely for her "extravagant" spending on charities. So Matilda gave them all her inheritance and left the court. But a few years later, she returned and again took an active part in ruling the kingdom and again became "extravagant" in helping her people.

Have you ever been "extravagant" and spent more money than others thought you should spend? Did you spend the money on things you wanted OR did you give it away like Matilda did? SOME people spend a lot of money on foolish fads and "extras" for themselves but give very little to help the poor and hungry. Maybe there would be fewer homeless and hungry people if MORE people were a little bit "extravagant" in helping others. What do you think?

Matthew

Some people might not LIKE this saint, since he was a TAX COLLECTOR! Others might like him because the name Matthew means "gift of God"!

Matthew lived at the

same time Jesus did, and people THEN did not like to pay taxes any better than TODAY'S people do! They often would have nothing to do with a man who earned his living by collecting taxes. They didn't want to talk to him, wouldn't invite him to parties, and probably even crossed the street when they saw him coming so they wouldn't have to speak to him!

Jesus, however, CHOSE Matthew to be one of his apostles. And Matthew was a very good apostle, preaching, and baptizing many. He also wrote the Gospel of Matthew in the Bible—and it has been read by millions of people through the centuries. So it turned out that THIS tax collector truly WAS a "gift from God"!

Do you ever JUDGE someone by the work he or she does? Would you be MORE impressed by someone who had a job as a doctor or a lawyer or a business executive than by someone who had a job as a tax collector or maybe even a garbage collector? Fortunately, God does not judge people by the jobs they have, the color of their skin, or the size of their bank accounts! It's GOOD to have ambition and want to get the best job you can get, but it's even more important to want to DO the best job you can with WHATEVER job you have! So whatever job you have to do today, try to do your BEST—even if you have to "tax" your mind or muscle!

Matthias

Here's a saint who might be called a Johnny-come-lately, second choice, or better-late-than-never! And he was proud of it!

You know that when Jesus was on earth, he chose twelve special friends or apostles who would continue his work. BUT one of the twelve—Judas—betrayed Jesus, and then there were only eleven. So the apostles decided to choose someone to take Judas' place—and they chose Matthias.

Since Matthias had not known Jesus personally, he must have been eager to hear the other apostles tell all about what Jesus was like and what he said and did. And then Matthias tried to follow that example and became a very good apostle, telling OTHER people about Jesus.

Matthias didn't mind at all being second choice, taking the place of someone else. He was just happy to be one of THE CHOSEN!

Would YOU have liked to sit around with the apostles and hear them talk about Jesus and tell what he was like and what he did and said? Well, you can do that today! You can read the Bible! That's where the apostles wrote it all down! And then you—like Matthias—can tell OTHER people! Because you, too, have been CHOSEN—to be a friend of Jesus!

Monica

How long Lord? How long?

Here's a saint who had a bad-tempered husband and mother-in-law PLUS a smart but LAZY son. What a combination!

In spite of the aggravations of her family (or maybe because of them), Monica became a saint—and her son did too!

No matter how difficult things were at home, Monica was always patient and sweet to everyone, and she prayed constantly for her husband and son to change. After many years, her husband finally followed her example and became a Christian before he died. But her son would NOT.

By this time, Monica's son, Augustine, had left their home in North Africa and traveled to Italy, where he had a very successful career and many friends, but he lived an evil life. Saint Monica continued to pray for him and after seventeen years of prayer, Augustine not only changed his life and was baptized but he became one of the greatest saints of the Church. (See page 25 to learn more about Augustine.)

Monica did NOT become famous because her son was famous. Monica became a famous saint because of her patience, her prayers, and her persistence. She did NOT give up. Today, people expect prayers to be answered INSTANTLY—the same way they get instant coffee, instant pizza, or instant TV. But God does not always answer in a hurry. So don't try to rush God. When you pray for something, be patient, be persistent—and don't give up!

Patrick

This saint had a dream—and it changed his life!

When Patrick was only sixteen years old, he was captured in a raid and taken by ship to Ireland, where he was sold as a slave! He was put to work as a shepherd, and for seven lonely years on a desolate mountaintop, he cared for sheep and prayed and longed for home. Then one night he had a dream in which he was given "directions" about how to escape!

It must have been a doozie of a dream because the next day, Patrick decided to set out on the long journey to freedom. He walked TWO HUNDRED miles before he came to the seashore and found a ship which would take him home.

BUT once he got home, Patrick kept thinking about Ireland! He had liked the Irish people and felt sorry for them because they knew nothing about Jesus or his Church. Finally, Patrick returned to Ireland, taking twenty priests and deacons with him. Before long, so many people had been instructed and joined the Church that Ireland became known as a Catholic country.

> Do you ever have funny dreams when you go to sleep at night? Well, what about the daytime—do you ever have "daydreams," wishes, hopes, goals, for the future? Most people don't get "instructions" in a dream; they have to make their own plans and schemes for the future. So, do some daydreaming today about your OWN goals and hopes. You know what they say—if you DON'T have a dream, then you'll never have a dream come true!

Paula

This saint was a happy housewife. She and her husband were considered an ideal couple. They had five children and a very happy family. When her husband died, Paula mourned him greatly; but instead of spending the rest of her life weeping, she decided to spend it working for the Church.

At first, Paula worked in Rome, where her family lived. Later she traveled with one of her sons to the Holy Land and built a monastery and a convent there. Since she was from a noble family, Paula had money, and she used most of it in helping to build many churches. She turned from weeping to worthwhile work and lived a successful and saintly life!

Did you ever have something happen that made you so sad you thought you would never be happy again? Everybody gets sad sometimes, but nobody has to STAY sad. There are so many happy things in the world—bubble gum and bubble baths, sparkly soda pop and sparkly friends, ice-cream sundaes and all-day-off Saturdays, a warm bed to sleep in and a good book to read and the for-sure, no-doubt-about-it knowledge that God loves you. The next time you feel sad, think about that and get glad.

Peregrine Laziosi

Here's a saint who kept on the move! Legend says that he never sat down for thirty years! Can you imagine that?

When Peregrine was a young man, he had an argument with a priest who was a representative of the pope, and Peregrine punched him in the face. The priest turned the other cheek—just as Jesus had done in the Bible. This so surprised Peregrine that he decided he better change his hot-tempered ways.

Later Peregrine, too, became a priest and decided that he should always be working toward perfection and never SIT DOWN! He became known for his holiness and the way he preached and helped those in trouble. Peregrine lived to be eighty years old, so evidently keeping on the move was good for him!

> SIT DOWN today! Close your eyes and pretend you have a magic carpet that can take you anywhere you want to go. (You DO have a magic carpet, you know—it's called your imagination!) Now where will you go—to Rome, to the Holy Land, to Mars? Wherever you go, when you get there, it will be a place that was made by God! And you won't have to travel alone because God will go with you. Isn't that a happy thought? No matter how far you go or how you travel, God will always keep you company—so you will never have to be alone or lonely!

Peter Claver

Here's a saint who was known as the "slave of the slaves"! He was born in Spain and graduated with honors from the University of Barcelona before he became a Jesuit priest and went to work in Cartagena (now known as Colombia), which was then a central port, or "clearinghouse," for the slave trade.

Conditions there were terrible, but Peter stayed where the slaves stayed, took them food and medicine, and tried to get the authorities to treat them more kindly. Once he became known as their friend, he took along a band of interpreters who could speak African dialects and tried to tell the slaves about

Christianity. Even though their situation was desperate, he tried to give them some degree of self-respect by telling them how Jesus had died for them and how God loved them as his children.

It is said that in his forty years of work with the slaves, Peter baptized THREE HUNDRED THOUSAND! He has become an inspiration to African-American Catholics all through the Americas.

> Who do you know who is an INSPIRATION—a teacher, a relative, a friend? Who has been the greatest inspiration in YOUR life? Maybe it's someone you see every day, or maybe it's someone you've never even spoken to, someone you've only read about. Whoever it is, why don't you TELL that person! If you would be embarrassed to say thank you in person, you could write an ANONYMOUS letter to your own special "inspiring" person. It will be your SECRET— but a thank you like that could be an "inspiration" to the one who's been an inspiration to YOU!

Peter Mary Chanel

Some people might have called this saint "teacher's pet" because he was a great favorite of his teachers in school. BUT he was also well liked by his fellow students!

Peter began working as a shepherd boy when he was only seven years old, but the parish priest noticed how intelligent he was and asked Peter's parents if they would let him attend the parish school. Peter was a "model student" there and also in the seminary where he studied later.

After Peter became a priest, he asked to work in the missions and was sent with a small group of missionaries to one of the islands in the Pacific. The natives welcomed them, and as soon as the priests learned the native language and began to teach, many natives asked to be baptized.

This made the chieftain jealous and suspicious of the missionaries. But when the chief's SON decided to become a Catholic, that jealousy turned to HATE, and the chief sent a band of warriors to attack the priests. Peter was killed and became a martyr (someone who has died for the Faith), but his death was a victory! When the people heard what had happened,

even MORE asked to be baptized, and within a few months, the whole island was Catholic!

In the history of the Church—and even in recent years—many brave men and women have given their lives to spread the word of God. Few people are ever asked to make such a GREAT sacrifice, but the martyrs can be a shining example to YOU and to all other Christians, who are asked only to make SMALL sacrifices.

Peter Nolasco

When Peter was only fifteen years old, he inherited a FORTUNE! Wow! A teenager with a fortune. What do you guess he did with it?

Well, in Peter's day—thirteenth-century France—there were no fancy sports cars or designer jeans—but there WERE many rich things he could have bought with his money. Instead, Peter decided to spend the money for RANSOM—to buy people!

You've probably heard about kidnappers who will take someone hostage and then demand a RANSOM—a lot of money—before they will free the captive. Well, in Peter's time, most of Spain was ruled by the Moors, and you COULD call them kidnappers. They

HATED Christians, so they would capture Christians and then make them work as slaves!

Peter had heard about this and felt very sorry for the slaves, so he got the idea that MAYBE the Moors would take a RANSOM for their slaves. Peter traveled from France to Barcelona, Spain, and was able to "make a deal" with the Moors to BUY BACK some Christian slaves! When others heard about this, many decided to help Peter, and they named their group "The Order of Our Lady of Ransom." They made it their life-work to raise money and then RANSOM Christian slaves!

If YOU won a sweepstakes or the lottery and suddenly had a FORTUNE, what would you do with it? Even if you just have a small allowance now, your money might SEEM like a fortune to the poorest people in other parts of the world. Did you know that SOME people give a portion of all the money they get to help others? Every time they get a dollar, they give maybe five cents or ten cents to the Church or to some charity. This is called tithing. What do you think of that idea?

Philip of Zell

Crime does not pay! It's not good to steal anything from anybody, but it could be even worse to steal something from a saint! Some thieves who tried it with Saint Philip found that out!

Philip lived way out in the woods as a hermit, spending his days working in his vegetable garden and praying. The people around there knew that he was a very holy man and often came to visit him and ask for his help and advice. Even the king of that area sometimes came to visit Philip and talk with him about holy things. But one night Philip had a different kind of visitor.

Thieves came and stole the two oxen Philip used to help him plow his garden. All night long the thieves wandered around with those oxen, trying to find their way out of the woods—but for SOME REASON, they couldn't find a way out! When morning came, they were right back where they had started—in front of Philip's little house!

The thieves were so surprised that they fell to their knees and asked the saint to forgive them. Of course, Philip did, but he also invited them in, fed them,

treated them like guests, and then sent them on their way.

Don't you bet those thieves learned a lesson and never tried to steal anything from anybody again?

Did anyone ever steal something from YOU? It's a terrible thing to steal anything from anybody. Today would be a good time for YOU to "steal away" for a little quiet time alone. Don't listen to music or TV or the radio or somebody's else's voice. Just get very quiet, all alone somewhere, and listen. You might hear the wind blow or a bird chirp. You might imagine what it was like for Philip to live waaaay out in the woods, away from all the noise of the nearest village, alone with the wind and the birds and with God. You might even hear God speak softly, inside your head or your heart, to YOU.

Philippine Duchesne

This saint went from a life of leisure in France to a log cabin in America! She got seasick crossing an ocean, dragged a cow across a frozen river, spent time with the Indians, and became a pioneer in education!

Philippine had a nice life with her family in France, but she wanted to be a missionary, and she ESPECIALLY wanted to teach American Indians! So she became a nun and left her home to sail to America. On the long ocean voyage, she was seasick and homesick —but never discouraged.

Once in America, Philippine faced many hardships—living in a log cabin where the snow blew through cracks in the wall, trying to write letters in a room so cold the ink FROZE, and getting supplies for her Sisters and students even if it meant dragging that milkcow over the ice when it didn't want to cross the river to "join" her convent!

Mother Duchesne became an education pioneer when she opened the FIRST FREE school west of the Mississippi River. After that, she and other Sacred Heart Sisters opened many schools in the frontier towns of America—and their convents and schools still flourish today.

Mother Duchesne spent many years struggling against almost impossible odds, pioneering education in America, but FINALLY

she was able to turn over her work to others. THEN, when she was seventy-one years old, she was able to realize her dream of working for the American Indians. At her age, learning their language was difficult, but the Indians understood her language of love and dedication. They honored and revered her and called her "the woman who prays always."

Would you like to be a PIONEER? There are many fields where people are pioneering today—medicine, technology, computers, SPACE! The world is always waiting to welcome people with new ideas, new solutions, new possibilities. Dream today of how YOU could be a pioneer—and then make plans to do it! (And if you know someone who HAD a dream but was never able to realize it, tell him or her it's never too late! Mother Duchesne had to wait until she was seventy-one years old, but she DID achieve her dream!)

Raymund of Peñafort

Gotta go to work!

Do you know anyone who is sixty-five years old? That's the age when many people decide to quit their jobs and "retire" from their work. And that's what Saint Raymund did. But then he lived and worked thirty-five more years—until he was ONE HUNDRED YEARS OLD!

Raymund had a very busy young life working in Spain and then working for the pope in Rome and then back in Spain again. When he was sixty-three years old, he was slowing down a bit, happily living a quiet life, but THEN he was elected to be the HEAD of an Order of priests. He didn't want this job but took it and worked very hard and made many changes in the next two years. Then, when he was sixty-five, he asked to resign because of his "old" age.

Little did anyone know that he would go on working for the Church for another thirty-five years. In his later years, most of his work was done with the Moors in Spain, trying to get them to convert to Christianity. In the year 1256 (when he was eighty-one years old), he wrote to say that TEN THOUSAND Moors had been baptized. Not bad for a man who had retired years before because of his "old" age!

Would you like to work until you are a hundred years old? Would you like to LIVE to be a hundred years old? Well, the most important thing is not how LONG you live but HOW you live! Saint Raymund used every one of his years wisely and well. And you can do the same. Make the MOST of today. Learn something NEW today. Do something FUN today. Do something GOOD today. Say a prayer today. Live EVERY day that way—and you will have a happy life!

Richard of Wyche

There's a very popular song from a Broadway show that includes the words, "Day by day...day by day...Oh dear Lord...three things I pray...to know thee more clearly....love thee more dearly...follow thee more nearly...day by day...." Do you know that song? Well, would you have guessed that those words came from a prayer written by this saint?

Richard was the Bishop of Chichester in England during the reign of King Henry III. He was known as a good bishop who was very charitable to the poor—and he would have been very surprised to know that his words would one day be sung on radio and TV all around the world!

Today would be a good day for YOU to sing a song. Why? Because EVERY day is a good day to sing a song, to be joyful, AND to do your best to know, love, and follow the Lord!

Rita of Cascia

This saint had a husband who was so insulting and had such a violent temper that he was the terror of the whole neighborhood! For many years, Rita was patient and kind to him, praying that he would change some day—and finally he did! His conscience began to waken, and he realized how mean he had been and was sorry for the way he had acted. He came to Rita and begged her forgiveness for all the sorrow he had caused her.

Rita was so grateful and thought they could now have a happier life. But just a short time later, her husband was murdered (probably by an enemy he had made with his violent temper!). After that, Rita joined a convent and continued to be kind and gentle with the Sisters there and with the people they helped—just as she had been with her troublesome husband.

Today, there are doctors and treatment centers to help those who are abusive to others, but in Saint Rita's time, the only help was in prayer. If anyone is ever abusive to YOU, you should pray for that person, but you should ALSO tell someone you trust—a relative, teacher, counselor, or pastor—and ask for help. Say a prayer today for all the people in the world who are being mistreated or abused.

Robert Bellarmine

Do you ever wish you were as tall as a seven-foot basketball player so you could see over and above instead of between and around other people's heads? Well, maybe this saint did too—because Robert was so short, he had to stand on a stool in the pulpit when he spoke so people could see and hear him!

Although Robert was so short in stature, he was so long on achievements that it would take this whole book just to tell about them all! But here's a SHORT list of some things he did: He wrote two catechisms (books to teach people about the Catholic religion), was a university professor and lecturer, became a cardinal and head of the Vatican library, and was a friend of the astronomer Galileo. He wrote so many scholarly and theological books that his enemies suggested a whole group of learned men must have collaborated on them, since it would be hard to believe that this could be the work of just one man—and one very short man, at that!

If you ever feel "short"—of money, brain power, athletic ability, or just height—remember Robert Bellarmine. Someone once said that "good things come in small packages," and it was certainly true with this saint. So remember, no matter how short, tall, skinny, wide, brainy, sporty, or whatever you are, you are SPECIAL because God made you and loves you. Think tall, think good, think God! With prayer and work, you can achieve great heights!

Roch

Say ahh...

Could a rock become a saint? No, but a Roch could—and did! Way back in the fifteenth century, Roch was already a popular saint in France and Italy, but for some reason, no one ever wrote down a history of his life, so we don't know very much about him. We DO know that he was very kind and good. He nursed many sick people when a terrible plague hit Italy—and he was able to cure many of them.

One legend says that he once caught this terrible plague himself and since he didn't want anyone else to have to take care of him, he dragged himself out in the woods to die. But a dog found him and brought him some food! Then the dog's master found him and cared for him. Roch recovered and went back to nursing and cured many more people and even cured some of their sick cattle! That's why he is the patron of cattle and also of people who have contagious diseases.

Did you ever have a "contagious" disease—something that other people can "catch," like the measles or chicken pox or maybe even a cold? It's no fun being even a little bit sick, so it must be awful to be sick with something really serious. No one catches the plague anymore, but there are still a lot of people in the hospitals with serious illnesses. Why don't you get your friends to help you make some hand-drawn "get well" cards and then put them in a big envelope and mail it to a local hospital? Include a note saying, "Please give these cards to some really sick people who don't usually get cards." Won't they be SURPRISED?

123

Rose of Lima

With a name like that, you might guess that Saint Rose is the patron of gardeners and florists! Not only that, Rose loved to do gardening work and even LIVED in a garden!

She was born in Lima, Peru, and was a very beautiful young lady—but she didn't like anyone to notice her beauty. When her parents lost all their money because of an unsuccessful mining venture, Rose wanted to help them. She grew food and earned money for them by working in the garden all day and by sewing late into the night. Her parents wanted her to get married, but Rose refused.

Instead, she continued with her work but moved out of their house into a little hut in the garden. There, she spent all her free time in prayer. Many people made fun of her for doing this but many others came to ask her to pray for THEM—and many of them received happy answers to those prayers.

Do YOU ever pray for somebody else? It's good to pray for yourself—when you need help or are afraid or feel sorry for something bad you've done or want to say thanks for a special blessing. But today, why don't you pray for somebody else? Think now. Do you know someone who might need help? Say a prayer—or LOTS of prayers—for him or her today.

Rose of Viterbo

What would you think of a twelve-year-old girl who PREACHED up and down her street? That's what this Saint Rose did.

When she was only eight years old, Rose dreamed that she saw Mary, our Blessed Mother, and Mary told her she should set a good example for her neighbors, both by word and work. Rose DID set a good example by being a very good, prayerful little girl. But when she was about twelve years old, an emperor took over Viterbo, where Rose and her family lived—and this emperor was AGAINST the pope. The people of Viterbo were afraid of the emperor and were not doing anything to voice their support for the pope. So that's when Rose began to preach up and down the streets, telling people they should be AGAINST the emperor and FOR the pope.

Crowds began to gather at her house to hear her, and Rose continued to preach for the pope for about two years. By then, friends of the emperor had become enraged, and they tried to get the chief magistrate of the town to have Rose put to death as a danger to the state! The magistrate was a just man and refused to do this, but he DID have Rose and her family banished from Viterbo. They had to leave their home and move to another city! But in a few years, the emperor died, and they were able to return home—where Rose continued to live a good and holy life and "set a good example for her neighbors by both word and work."

Do YOU set a good example for your neighbors? You know you don't have to go up and down the street preaching to do that! You can do little helpful things for your neighbors—help a tired mom carry in bags of groceries from the car to the house, read a book to a younger child who can't read yet, run an errand for an older person, be polite and spend time visiting with someone who's lonely, offer to help with yard work or housework. There are LOTS of little ways you can set a good example, just by acting like you think Jesus would EXPECT a Christian to act. What could you do TODAY to set a good example for a neighbor?

Sabas

This saint did NOT have a happy childhood.

His father was an army officer who was sent to Egypt for a long tour of duty, and Sabas was left to live with an uncle and aunt. The aunt was so mean to Sabas that he RAN AWAY when he was only eight years old and went to live with another uncle. The two uncles began to fight and even drew up lawsuits over Sabas because they both wanted his father's MONEY. So Sabas ran away AGAIN—but this time he went to a monastery! And he stayed there for ten years.

Then he traveled to Jerusalem and lived in a different monastery. Finally, he founded a "laura"—a place where each monk would live alone in a little hut during the week but would join all the other monks on Saturday and Sunday to pray together. Men came from many countries to join this laura that was located in the wild, desolate area between Jerusalem and the Dead Sea. It became very famous, and many saints lived there at different times. In fact, TODAY—more than fourteen hundred years after Saint Sabas died—monks STILL live in the "laura" he began!

Would YOU like to live in a wild and desolate place? Or would you rather live in a busy, bustling city? It doesn't matter WHERE you live—just HOW you live! Wherever you are, you can live a happy life AND a prayerful life. So if you haven't already started, start TODAY—be happy and prayerful!

Salome

We don't know a lot about this saint, but what we DO know is plenty!

Salome is one of the women mentioned in the New Testament of the Bible. She was the wife of Zebedee and the mother of TWO apostles—James and John! Not only that, Salome was one of the women who followed Jesus and was standing with Mary at the foot of the cross when Jesus died.

All this makes Salome a very special lady! The little we know about her tells us that she was a good wife and mother and a faithful follower of Jesus. What else do we need to know!

Some saints have done daring deeds, braved torture, fought crusades, or built monasteries and churches. But here's a lady who simply did her best to be a good person. She must have been a good mother to have TWO sons chosen by Jesus to be his apostles. And she must have been a very brave woman to NOT run away when Jesus was crucified, to stay with him and his mother on that terrible day. So you see—a saint can be an ordinary person who loves God and shows it by the way she or he lives an ordinary, everyday life. That's how one of YOUR friends or relatives could be a saint. That's how YOU could be a saint too!

Scholastica

If you read about Benedict in this book, then you know that Saint Scholastica had a famous brother. But Benedict also had a famous sister!

Just as Benedict founded a monastery for men, Scholastica founded a "nunnery" for women. This religious house was one of the first established for women in Europe, and it made a great difference in the lives of many women.

The women of that day did not have many choices in life. If a girl was born into a poor family, she became a servant or married a poor man and struggled to raise a family, with no prospects of ever "bettering" the life of herself or her children. If she was born into a royal family, she lived a royal lifestyle that was often very structured with certain rules to be followed in the court or castle. Many women had to marry men they didn't even know because the marriage would make a proper "royal connection" for the two families.

Few women learned to read or write, and there was very little opportunity for a woman to live a useful life outside of castle, court, or home. Scholastica's convents—and those that were opened in later years—offered women a haven where they could find education, companionship, a life of prayer and work, and an honorable alternative to marriage (especially "arranged" marriages to strangers!).

Did YOU ever know anyone who had joined a convent? Did you ever have a teacher who was a nun? All through the years, since the early days of the Church, many women have joined convents. Some of them became famous as the heads of hospitals, schools, orphanages, colleges, or held other important jobs. Some did NOT become famous but DID live very happy, useful lives. The Church owes a great debt of gratitude to all these holy women who gave their lives to serve the Church. Today, the Church NEEDS more young women like that. Say a prayer today that many young women in YOUR generation will choose to serve God by joining a convent or maybe even beginning a NEW one like Saint Scholastica did!

Sennen and Abdon

What? You never heard of these saints—and you think their names sound like mouthwash? Well, wash your mouth out with soap! These two brave saints were Persian noblemen who were

arrested for the terrible "crime" of being Christians! They were put in chains and taken to Rome, where they were told to give up this "silly" religion of Christianity and honor the Romans' false gods. It would have been sooo easy.

Since they were noblemen, Sennen and Abdon probably had plenty of money to live the "good life"—and wanted to keep it that way. And all they had to do was agree with the Romans and say Christianity was a no-good religion and they didn't even want to be Christians anymore. That would have been the SMART thing to do, wouldn't it? Or would it?

Sennen and Abdon believed in Jesus Christ and his religion with all their heart. They could not betray their faith. So what did the Romans do? They got really mad and had their soldiers kill the two brave noblemen. Sennen and Abdon died rather than give up their Christian faith. Do you think any of your Christian friends would be that brave? Would you?

You'll probably never get "put in chains," but there WILL be LOTS of times when people will tell you that Christianity is a "silly" religion and you should give it up. They'll even tell you God doesn't love you (which is really "silly" because God DOES love you). They'll tell you to do your own thing instead of that dumb Christianity thing. What will YOU tell them?

Severinus Boethius

You have probably never heard of Boethius, but A LOT of people heard about him and admired him once upon a time in Rome.

Boethius grew up in an interesting home at an exciting and dangerous time in history. His father was an important public official and guests were always at their house, talking about the things happening in the world at that time—the crumbling of the old Roman Empire, the beginning of new countries, the news and views of their city. Boethius loved to read and study and to hear all this conversation.

Boethius wanted to share all his knowledge with others, but few people at that time could read, and those few could only read Latin.

Boethius studied the Greek language so he could read all about the ideas of the great Greek thinkers like Aristotle and Plato. And THEN Boethius translated into Latin what he had learned so the people of Rome could also learn what he did. They were fascinated to hear all those new ideas about politics, music, science, mathematics, philosophy, and theology. And they were grateful to Boethius for his work.

For HUNDREDS of years, there were no other Latin translations from the Greek except the ones Boethius had done! Boethius especially liked to learn about God, and he wrote a book about the Trinity that is still read by some today. Another of his books was a "bestseller" for a THOUSAND years and was read by almost every well-educated person in Europe for many, many years. Boethius was only forty-four years old when he died, but in that short time, he had achieved a great deal. The good life he led and his writing inspired thousands of people for hundred of years, and he is still an inspiration today, more that fifteen hundred years after his death.

Today's computers, TV, and INSTANT communication make it easy to learn about what people are doing and thinking around the world. And yet we often hear only the BAD news instead of hearing the kinds of things Boethius wrote about—new ideas in education, philosophy, and religion. Look at TODAY's newspaper, and see how many GOOD news stories you can find. Then see how many stories you can find about God!

Stanislaus Kostka

Do you have an older brother who is always picking on you or making fun of you—or do you have a FRIEND with an older brother like that? Well, that's the kind of brother Saint Stanislaus had!

Stanislaus and his brother, Paul, were sons of a senator of Poland and had a private tutor who taught them at home until Paul was sixteen and Stanislaus was fourteen. Then their father sent them to attend a school in Vienna. Paul was high-spirited and just wanted to have a good time, but Stanislaus was serious and studious and wanted to become a priest. Paul couldn't understand this so he teased and made fun of Stanislaus for two years. Stanislaus couldn't ask his father for help because his father didn't want him to become a priest either.

Finally, Stanislaus decided that he would WALK to Rome—a three-hundred-fifty-mile trip—and ask to enter the Jesuit seminary there. It wasn't long before Paul found out his brother was gone and set out to bring him back, but he couldn't find him. Stanislaus had made his way to a college where a priest took him in and then helped him continue his journey to Rome.

Stanislaus was accepted by the Jesuits in Rome and was very happy there, but the summer heat of Rome was hard on him, and he began to have fainting spells and became ill. When his father heard that Stanislaus had joined the Jesuits in spite of his advice against it, he was furious and sent Paul to bring his brother home. But travel was very slow in those days, and when Paul arrived in Rome, angry and ready to tease his brother some more and demand that he return with him, he was too late. His brother had died. The shock was so terrible, Paul began to rethink the way he had acted. He began to be sorry for the way he had treated Stanislaus, for all the teasing and all the mean things he had said to him. Paul never got over the shock. He spent the rest of his life wishing he had been nicer to his little brother.

To everyone's surprise, when Paul was sixty years old, he decided to join the Jesuits—just as his little brother had done many years before.

> Did you ever act mean to someone in your family? Well, don't feel too bad—even SAINTS have relatives who make fun of them. But that doesn't mean you have to keep it up! It's SOOOO easy to tease and make fun of somebody else, but it's not so much fun when somebody else makes fun of YOU! So the next time you start to say mean things, think how you would feel if somebody said mean things to you. Think of Saint Stanislaus and then, don't tease—please?

Tarasius

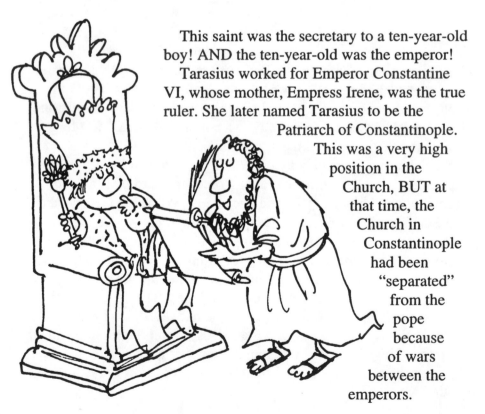

This saint was the secretary to a ten-year-old boy! AND the ten-year-old was the emperor! Tarasius worked for Emperor Constantine VI, whose mother, Empress Irene, was the true ruler. She later named Tarasius to be the Patriarch of Constantinople. This was a very high position in the Church, BUT at that time, the Church in Constantinople had been "separated" from the pope because of wars between the emperors.

Tarasius accepted the new post ONLY on the condition that he be allowed to hold a council and settle differences so THAT part of the Church could be "reconciled" with the pope.

After holding a successful council, Tarasius continued to work very hard and pray very hard to reform his clergy and his people. He was very charitable and visited every "poor house" and hospital in the city to be sure no poor person would be overlooked.

Tarasius went from being the secretary to the head of a country to being the head of that country's Church! And he did both jobs well.

Do you know what kind of work a secretary does? Some secretaries have very important jobs. They take notes at big meetings, schedule appointments, type letters dictated by the "boss," and handle all the little OR big chores necessary to keep an office running smoothly. Would YOU like to be a secretary? Why don't you try being secretary of your HOUSE for a day and handle as many things as you can to keep it running smoothly!

Veronica

No one knows much about this saint, but the one fact we DO know is that her name was NOT Veronica!

Here's the story. Suppose you saw a criminal coming down the street with a crowd following him and the criminal looked real sad and his face was all smeared with perspiration and blood, and THEN a woman dashed out of the crowd and gave the poor man a cloth to wipe his face. Well, that's what happened the day Jesus was crucified.

Jesus had been condemned as a CRIMINAL and was carrying his cross to the place where he would be crucified. Naturally, he looked real sad and the day was hot so he was perspiring and his head was bleeding from the crown of thorns. But instead of trying to help him, the crowd was yelling and making fun of him. And THEN this ONE woman felt so sorry for him that she took the veil (scarf) from her head and ran out and gave it to Jesus so he could wipe his face. And when Jesus gave the veil back to her, she looked and saw it had the IMAGE of Jesus' face on it!

No one really knows WHO the woman was or what happened to her after that, but legend says that she became a Christian, and before she died, she gave the veil to Pope Clement. So why do we call her Veronica? Well, that's the Latin for "true image"—and since Jesus left the true image of his face on her veil, she became known as Veronica!

What do YOU think Jesus really looked like? Close your eyes and try to imagine how he looked that day when he saw Veronica. THEN try to imagine how he looks today when HE looks at YOU!

Vincent de Paul

Captured by pirates, sent on a secret mission to France, appointed chaplain to a queen—these were some of the adventures of Vincent de Paul, a saint who led an exciting and sometimes dangerous life.

When he was young, Vincent was captured by pirates and SOLD as a slave. Two years later, he managed to escape and returned to Rome to continue his studies. But then he was sent on the secret mission and later was named to be the chaplain to the queen. He also became a teacher in the household of a count who was the general in charge of galleys—long boats equipped with many oars that were manned by slaves. (There were NO motorboats way back then!) Of course, the galley slaves lived very sad lives, and Vincent began to minister to them.

Although he was friends with royalty and nobility, Vincent's whole life became devoted to serving slaves, peasants, and the poor. Soon he had many helpers, and their work spread to far-flung countries. Vincent's life was exciting, but even more important, it was a life devoted to helping others!

Do you think YOUR life is exciting? Do you think it WILL BE some day? Even more important, do you think your life will be worthwhile—a life of service, a life of goodness, a life that accomplishes something? What could you DO to be of service, to help others some day—OR what could you do THIS day?

Zeno

Zeno had an unusual name AND an unusual nickname. He is sometimes called the "saint who smiles"! Hopefully, A LOT of saints smiled, but Zeno got this name because there is a statue of him in the basilica in Verona, Italy—and it is a statue of a happy, smiling bishop.

This statue is notable because so MANY sculptors made statues of saints looking very serious and somber—which is probably not the way they looked at all! Maybe Zeno's sculptor had heard stories of how this bishop could smile even when he had serious problems. Zeno DID have problems because during his time as bishop, he had to defend the Church against many heresies and pagan superstitions. Zeno was a good pastor to his people, and he taught them they should always be kind and give hospitality and charity to all.

If someone made a statue of YOU, would they picture you as smiling—or as frowning, pouting or grouching? Look at yourself in a mirror today and think about the way your face USUALLY looks. Does it usually look happy? Does it usually look the way you WANT people to think of you? If it doesn't, maybe you better put a smile onto that face!

138

Zephyrinus (Pope)

This sounds like the name of a spaceship instead of a saint! But guess who this saint was? He was a pope—Pope Zephyrinus!

In fact, Zephyrinus became pope in the year 199—not much more than a hundred years after Jesus died. This made Zephyrinus one of the earliest popes in the almost-new Catholic Church.

Pope Who?

Did you know that *zephyr* is another name for a gentle breeze? Maybe Zephyrinus was like a gentle breeze in the Church. Is YOUR personality more like a gentle breeze or a wild wind? The world needs BOTH—gentle breezes to bring peace and contentment and wild winds to blow in fresh air and fresh ideas. Tell God thanks today for all the VARIETY in his world and in his people.

Zita

This saint went to work as a maid when she was only twelve years old! And she continued to work for the SAME family for forty-eight years!

At first, the other servants did NOT like Zita because she gave what little money she had to those who were even poorer than she was, and she prayed a lot, so they thought she was trying to be a

"goodie-goodie." After a while though, they realized Zita really WAS good.

In addition to her "saintly" ways, Zita was also a hard worker and always did her job well. She said, "A servant is not pious if she is not industrious. Work-shy piety is sham piety." Through the years, Zita became a friend and confidante of ALL those in the household where she worked, and she was a great favorite of the children.

Are YOU a hard worker? What kind of work do you like to do best? In the house...in the yard...at school...in front of the TV? Well, nobody can work ALL the time! They say all work and no play makes Jack a dull boy or Jacqueline a dull girl. But all play and NO work makes Jack a stupid boy or Jacqueline a stupid girl! So try to do SOME of each—a little work, a little play—each and EVERY day!

When the Saints Come Marching In, Which Ones Will Get Your Vote?

My favorite saint's name is _____

Because _____

My favorite saint's story is the one about _____

Because _____

The saint's name I wish I had been named is _____

Because _____

My friends who were named for saints include _____

My relatives who were named for saints include _____

The saint I think was the funniest is _____

Because _____

The saint I would like to learn more about is _____

Because _____

The saint I would most like to be like is _____

Because _____

My favorite "fun fact" in this book is _____

Is Your Name on This List?

How many people do you think have been "officially" named as saints? In one dictionary of the saints, there are some FIVE THOUSAND listed! Many saints were canonized many years ago, but the Church is always discovering NEW saints—so many new names will probably be added to the list in YOUR lifetime!

Here is a list of just SOME of the saints who are NOT in this book. Can you find YOUR NAME on this list?

Aaron	Donald	Justus	Roger
Abraham	Dorothy	Kevin	Rupert
Adam	Edmund	Leonard	Samson
Adela	Eugenia	Leopold	Sebastian
Agnes	Faith	Lucy	Simeon
Barbara	Felix	Madeleine	Stephen
Bartholomew	Frederick	Marcella	Susanna
Boris	Gabriel	Mark	Sylvester
Brendan	Gerard	Martha	Teresa
Bruno	Gertrude	Maximus	Theodora
Cecilia	Guy	Michael	Thomas
Charles	Helen	Mildred	Timothy
Christina	Henry	Nicholas	Ursula
Christopher	Herman	Odilia	Valerian
Claudia	Hilary	Oswald	Verena
Clement	Hugh	Otto	Victor
Columba	Ida	Owen	Virgil
Conrad	Isaac	Pontian	Walter
Cornelius	Isabel	Procopius	Wilfrid
Daniel	Jane	Quentin	Winifred
David	Jordan	Raphael	Wolfgang
Dominica	Julia	Reginald	Zachary

Epilogue

This book will just give you a taste, an idea, a sampling, of the stories of the saints. It is much too small to list ALL the saints, so if you don't find your "name" saint here OR if you would like to know MORE about one of your favorite saints, don't stop here!

You can find more stories about the saints in the companion to this book, *365 Fun Facts for Catholic Kids.* But don't stop there either! Go to the library or a bookstore and look for a book that will tell you the REST of the story. And who knows? When you find more details and particulars of the lives of the saints, you might even find more "fun facts"!